URBAN scandinavian SEWING

18 Seasonal Projects for Modern Living

Includes Nordic Recipes & Traditions

Kirstyn Cogan

stashBOOKS®

an imprint of C&T Publishing

Text copyright © 2015 by Kirstyn Cogan

Photography and artwork copyright © 2015 by C&T Publishing, Inc.

PUBLISHER: Amy Marson

CREATIVE DIRECTOR: Gailen Runge

ART DIRECTOR/BOOK DESIGNER: Kristy Zacharias

EDITORS: S. Michele Fry and Joanna Burgarino

TECHNICAL EDITORS: Susan Hendrickson and Debbie Rodgers

PRODUCTION COORDINATOR: Jenny Davis

PRODUCTION EDITOR: Katie Van Amburg

ILLUSTRATOR: Jessica Jenkins

PHOTO ASSISTANT: Mary Peyton Peppo

STYLE PHOTOGRAPHY by Nissa Brehmer; INSTRUCTIONAL PHOTOGRAPHY by Diane Pedersen, unless otherwise noted

ADDITIONAL PHOTOGRAPHY by Shutterstock (snowy lane, page 9; hand heart, page 9; daffodil bike basket, page 55), iStock (Swedish Midsummer celebration, page 55; potato bowl, page 55), and Can Stock (snowy bikes, page 9).

Published by Stash Books, an imprint of C&T Publishing, Inc., P.O. Box 1456, Lafayette, CA 94549

Attention Copy Shops: Please note the following exception—publisher and author give permission to photocopy pages 79, 80, 86, 92, 93, and 98, and pattern pullout pages P1 and P2 for personal use only.

Attention Teachers: C&T Publishing, Inc., encourages you to use this book as a text for teaching. Contact us at 800-284-1114 or ctpub.com for lesson plans and information about the C&T Creative Troupe.

We take great care to ensure that the information included in our products is accurate and presented in good faith, but no warranty is provided nor are results guaranteed. Having no control over the choices of materials or procedures used, neither the author nor C&T Publishing, Inc., shall have any liability to any person or entity with respect to any loss or damage caused directly or indirectly by the information contained in this book. For your convenience, we post an up-to-date listing of corrections on our website (ctpub.com). If a correction is not already noted, please contact our customer service department at ctinfo@ctpub.com or at P.O. Box 1456, Lafayette, CA 94549.

Trademark (™) and registered trademark (®) names are used throughout this book. Rather than use the symbols with every occurrence of a trademark or registered trademark name, we are using the names only in the editorial fashion and to the benefit of the owner, with no intention of infringement.

Library of Congress Cataloging-in-Publication Data

Cogan, Kirstyn, 1963-

Urban Scandinavian sewing : 18 seasonal projects for modern living / Kirstyn Cogan.

    pages cm

ISBN 978-1-61745-015-0 (soft cover)

1. House furnishings--Scandinavia. 2. Sewing. I. Title.

TT387.C64 2015

646'.11--dc23

                                        2014029603

Printed in China

10 9 8 7 6 5 4 3 2 1

Dedication

I dedicate this book to my mom, Elaine Johnson. I would not be here writing this if it were not for your unwavering support of my creative path. Thank you for teaching me (by example) the fine art of perseverance and for making sure I know where I come from.

I love you more than words could ever say.

Acknowledgments

This book would not have seen the light of day if it weren't for the following people.

First, my husband, Wes Cogan—thank you from the bottom of my heart for all the hours of proofing (I'm sure my editors thank you, too) and for your constant support and patience through it all. It means the world to me. I love you always.

Second, I've been blessed to live in the same city as my amazing cousin Charlene Forslund, who shares my love of fabric crafting. I will never be able to thank you enough for the time, talent, and smiles you've contributed to making this book happen. I love you to the moon and back, Cuz! Thank you also to my dear uncle, Bruce Johnson; my sister, Marnie Johnson; and to Tim Forslund (as well as the extended Forslund tribe) for being my sounding board for recipes and keeping me tapped into my Scandinavian heritage. *Skol!*

A huge thank-you to Michelle Wagner, an amazing artist and friend, who stepped in so generously with her time and talent to take a few projects over the finish line.

My heartfelt thanks to the Stash Books staff for believing in my work and providing me with the opportunity to do this. Thank you, Roxane Cerda and Gailen Runge, for your fun, persistent encouragement to make a submission, and a special thank-you to my editors Michele Fry, Joanna Burgarino, and Susan Hendrickson for keeping me on track through the process. Thank you also to Kristy Zacharias and Nissa Brehmer for bringing the creative direction to life.

With deep gratitude, thank you to my dad, Jerome Johnson, who without question supported my creative path from day one and whose dedication for living a creative life is in my heart always.

Finally, I want to say thank you to my "Finnish sisters," Pia and Ulla, for opening their hearts and making us feel so much at home in Helsinki. This book is better because of our time together. I can't wait to do it again.

Contents

Introduction

I grew up in the sunny suburbs of San Francisco—a long way from my great-grandparents' homelands of Sweden and Finland. Finding a good tortilla was easy. Finding good *lefse* was hard. In spite of being separated from the "homeland" by geography and generations, we were (and still are) a typical Scandinavian family, especially during the holidays.

My folks had a thing for all things *mod*—especially modern Scandinavian furniture (and design in general). I suppose I couldn't help taking after them. It is with great pleasure that I share some of that love of Scandinavian design, sprinkled with a bit of family tradition, with you in *Urban Scandinavian Sewing*.

Throughout this book, the word *modern* has often been replaced with *urban* for a couple of reasons. First, what we identify as modern Scandinavian design is actually a direct result of the Industrial Revolution. During the late nineteenth century and the first half of the twentieth century, large numbers of people moved from the countryside to the cities and began producing everyday products en masse. Second, most of us actually live in urban areas today.

Urban Scandinavian design and craft is founded on the belief that good design should not be considered a luxury or associated with financial status, but should be available to everyone. Also, good design should be beautiful, functional, and made from sustainable, easily available resources. Urban Scandinavian design, however, is much more than a *look* or a *style*—it's also a philosophy, a simpler way of living. Simple living (whether by necessity or choice) has always been a hallmark of Scandinavian life. Scandinavian design ultimately reflects the cultural attitudes of the Scandinavian people—keep things uncomplicated, beautiful, and functional while being connected to what matters most.

It probably goes without saying that Scandinavian design (in all its genres) is naturally influenced by extreme seasonal changes. Winter and summer are the two most celebrated seasons throughout Scandinavia. In celebration of these extreme seasons, the book is divided into two sections: winter and summer—actually, Midsummer.

It is my sincere hope that the following projects bring some light to your darkest winter nights and some lighthearted happiness to your long summer days. Enjoy!

Kirstyn

WELCOME TO SCANDINAVIA

Illustration by Kirstyn Cogan

NIGHT AND DAY

Sometimes we consider our seasons to be not winter and summer but night and day. During the winter solstice, areas close to the Arctic Circle are, for a few days of the year, almost totally dark, with the sun never rising above the horizon. Of course, in the summer the opposite is true. There are a few days of the year when the sun doesn't quite seem to set.

To many, Scandinavia is a monoethnic region up north somewhere. Some folks even think it's a country. Several countries actually make up the region. And if you ask different people, they might list different countries! Denmark, Norway, and Sweden definitely. Finland and Iceland usually. Greenland, not so much. Sure, the people and the countries share some characteristics, a common heritage, and related—but not identical—languages, but they each have special features. When I think of them, here's what comes to mind.

ICELAND   The beloved puffin: It is one of the most popular birds in the world and comes from Iceland. • Many Icelanders believe in elves. • Hand-knit woolens are the most common gifts brought back from visits to Iceland. • This is the location of the world-famous Blue Lagoon, a huge geothermal spa where ocean water is heated by Mother Nature.

NORWAY   The cheese slicer was invented here! • Seagull eggs are a delicacy. Two to three times larger than a chicken egg, they are served boiled on flatbread with butter, salt, and pepper—and an ice-cold beer. • Two decorative crafts that come from Norway are rosemaling and Hardanger embroidery. • Norwegians are said to be born with skis attached to their feet. Although people have been using skis for more than 4,000 years, skiing first became a sport in Norway. • The word *ski* actually stems from an Old Norse word meaning *wood*.

DENMARK   The Danes are well known for their design of furniture, glass, and ceramics, but did you know that Denmark is also the home of Legos? • The beloved fairytale writer Hans Christian Andersen was a Dane; he wrote "The Ugly Duckling," "The Little Mermaid," and "The Emperor's New Clothes." • You're more likely to meet up with a Dane in a public café than be invited to his or her home (or personal space) unless you are a family member or very close friend. Personal space is personal.

SWEDEN   Food! *Fika* is a coffee/tea/pastry break taken (as often as possible) by Swedes and is a good opportunity to bond with friends. • Waffle Day is March 25 and Cinnamon Bun Day is October 4. On Fat Tuesday or (*Fettisdagen*), the *semla* (a cream puff) is the pastry of choice. Yes, national days dedicated to consuming favored treats guilt free—gotta love the Swedes! • Trick-or-treating on Easter? Yep, that's what it looks like. Kids dress up like witches—also known as Easter hags—and present you with a handmade Easter card in exchange for sweet treats! • Two things to keep in mind when you're invited to a Swede's home: Be on time and take your shoes off.

FINLAND   Ice swimming and wife-carrying races are popular pastimes. Finland is also one of the least corrupt and most peaceful states on earth, and has one of the best education systems in the world and the most heavy metal bands per capita. (I think the juxtaposition may be significant.) • Finns drink more coffee than any other people around the globe (which is hard for me to imagine, being from Seattle). • Nokia (the original cell phone company) and Angry Birds (the game) were both born here. • Finnish architect/designer Alvar Aalto is considered one of the most influential contributors to the Scandinavian modernist movement, and his furniture and glassware are still being produced today. • In 1951, Marimekko, a company known for its timeless, bold, and oh-so-incredibly-Finnish textiles, was started in Helsinki by Viljo and Armi Ratia when their oilcloth factory failed and was converted to a garment plant.

Winter

All over Scandinavia, the winter holidays are celebrated with lighthearted exuberance and warmth during this darkest part of the year. Frosty white snow, warm wool hats, and pink cheeks, along with hearty feasts of food and drink, are all sure signs of winter. It's also the best time of year to view the northern lights, or aurora borealis, which means "dawn of the north." The northern lights appear in the sky like an ethereal flowing river of ever-changing multicolored light (ranging from shades of red and yellow to green, blue, and violet).

As you might expect, ice skating, skiing, ice fishing, and even ice swimming are all popular outdoor activities in the winter throughout Scandinavia. But really there's no better time of the year to cozy up indoors for some serious stitch craft! It's no coincidence that crafting is such an integral part of Scandinavian living. So invite some friends over, light the candles, bake some bread, perch a tomte near all the action, and brew up some *glögg*. It's time to enjoy the winter sewing season!

Pieced Wool Scarf

Finished Size: Approximately 6½″ × 75″

It's easy to get funky with this simple pieced scarf—just stack a strip of wool on top of another and stitch! The result is not only a fashionably casual accessory, but the loose layers of wool make it nice and warm too.

Wool comes in a wide range of sizes (and shapes, if you are felting an old wool sweater). I list the basic amounts I used, but you can mix and match to get as funky and creative as you want. There are some *amazing* dyed wool sources out there (see Resources, page 110).

EASY WOOL FELTING

Felting wool at home is easy. Perhaps you have an old wool sweater you can't wear anymore or you found a great wool skirt at the local thrift store you'd like to felt. Just wash it in very hot water and dry it in the dryer. Repeat. Easy, huh? Wool felted from a sweater works great for projects like the Pieced Wool Scarf. Follow the project cutting list, or simply cut a variety of strips from ½″ to 4″ wide and have fun!

Materials

Felted wool, 6 colors: 7″ × 17″ piece of each

Coordinating thread

Optional but Helpful

Rotary cutter, clear Omnigrid ruler, and self-healing cutting mat

Cutting

Cut each color of wool into the following strips:

2 strips 1″ × 7″   1 strip 3″ × 7″

1 strip 2″ × 7″   1 strip 4″ × 7″

2 strips 2½″ × 7″

Make It

1. Arrange the strips in an order you find pleasing, mixing colors and sizes. Overlap the strips by about ¼″ (alternating the strips so that the second strip is on top of the first strip, the next is underneath the previous strip, and so on). Pin the strips in place.

TIP

Alternate your straight stitch with a zigzag stitch, or another decorative stitch, to add some funky flair. To add dimension, layer a thin strip (or two) on top of a wide strip. Attach with a zigzag or decorative stitch.

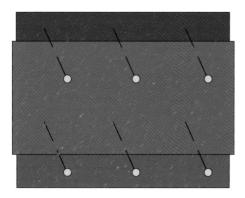

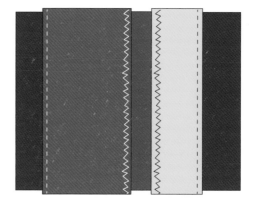

2. Stitch the strips together using a straight stitch. Be sure to lock your stitches, or backstitch, at the beginning and end of each seam. Keep sewing strips until the scarf is as long as you want it to be.

3. Trim any loose threads. Trim any uneven sides so that the scarf has a long, straight edge (a rotary cutter and ruler are helpful for this). Finish by sewing along each long side, ½″ from the edge, using any stitch you like.

4. *Optional:* Add an embellishment, such as a big wood button.

THE ST. LUCIA TRADITION

I often have friends ask me, "What's the deal with girls wearing lit candles on their heads?" In Sweden, December 13 was historically known as the winter solstice, but that date is now celebrated as St. Lucia's Day. Next to Christmas, it is the biggest celebration of the season.

Lucy means *light*. As the story goes, St. Lucia was a young girl killed for her Christian beliefs (dark, I know). "Lucy" would wear candles on her head (so she could have her hands free) and carry food through dark tunnels to persecuted Romans living in hiding.

Today, young girls dress up in white dresses with red sashes and wear lingonberry (kinda like cranberries, but teeny tiny) branches, symbolizing new life in winter, and crowns with candles. Yep, *real* lit candles on their heads for girls older than twelve. (Thankfully, little girls use electric candles.) Girls make *lussekatt* buns with saffron and topped with raisins and serve them to their parents. It's also common for groups of girls to visit hospitals and retirement homes in costume, singing carols and serving *pepparkakor* (ginger snap biscuits).

Seattle happens to have a large Scandinavian population (with Ballard being known as *the* Scandinavian neighborhood). One winter day a few years back, I happened to be sitting at a Starbucks in Ballard on St. Lucia Day, and in marched a group of "Lucia" girls with candles on their heads. Totally unexpected and majorly fun!

Felt Medallion Necklace

Finished Size: Felt pieces: ⅝″–2″; necklace strap: 12¼″ long

Making these groovy felt medallions is a bit like eating chips—it's hard to stop at one! They're not only easy to make and wear, but they make great gifts and holiday ornaments, too!

Materials

Makes 6–10 necklaces.

Wool or wool-blend felt, 3 colors: 12″ × 18″ sheet or ⅛ yard of each color (I used white, green, and dark gray.)

Hemp or cotton cord, 20-pound weight: 1 yard for each necklace

Metal washers: various sizes from ⅜″ to 2″, allowing 1 or 2 per necklace

Spray adhesive and liquid glue

Fabric-marking pen, several colors (Always test on a scrap of fabric before using. I recommend using FriXion pens.)

Coordinating thread

Hand-sewing and large-eyed chenille needles

Hammer and nail (¼″ head, just shy of ⅛″ thick)

Scrap wood

Optional but Helpful

Rolling pin

Chalk pencil (if you are using dark-colored felt)

Rubber needle puller

Needle threaders (for small and large needles)

Crewel wool embroidery thread

Embroidery needles

Beads or other embellishments

A Few Words about Felt Sheets

I recommend 100% wool or wool-blend felt (usually wool with rayon or bamboo). Wool and wool-blend felts look better and are biodegradable. Synthetic felt (or craft felt) is made from acrylic or polyester, which can melt when using a hot iron and is not biodegradable.

Felt is commonly sold in flat sheets or sometimes by the yard (see Resources, page 110). It is usually fairly thin, so in some projects I use spray adhesive to glue pieces together to make it thicker. If you are using 2mm-thick felt, you can skip the gluing. (Note: Some industrial felts are more than 2mm thick, but they are too heavy for our purposes.)

Make It

Cutting

Cut the felt in half. You should have 2 rectangles 9″ × 12″ if you are using felt sheets and 2 rectangles 9″ × width of fabric if you are using yardage (trim to 9″ × 12″).

TIP

Using a fabric-marking pen and the washer's center hole, trace a small felt circle in an accent color. This circle can be placed in the center of the washer for an extra pop of color. If you use a FriXion pen, the lines will disappear when you apply a hot iron to them—like magic!

TIP

Sometimes it is easier to use a couple of dots of liquid glue rather than spray adhesive to get the small pieces of felt in place.

1. If you are using 2mm felt, skip to Step 2. Place 1 rectangle of each color of felt on a flat surface protected with newsprint or paper. Following the manufacturer's instructions, spray with spray-on adhesive. (Be sure to do this in a well-ventilated area.) Place the second rectangle (the piece without adhesive) onto the sticky side and smooth it out. A rolling pin can help smooth out any bumps and bond the glued felt together.

2. Use a fabric-marking pen and the metal washers to trace circles onto the felt. Be sure to play around with several sizes. You'll have plenty of felt to work with, and some left over!

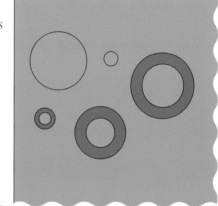

3. Cut out the felt circles. Blanket stitch (see Stitches, page 109) around each circle using doubled thread the same color as the circle to give it a nice finished look.

4. Stack the circles and determine how you want the finished piece to look. To make it reversible, add a washer to the back.

5. Spray adhesive to the back of each layer (including the washers) except the bottom, and place the felt circles from bottom to top in the order determined in Step 4. Let the adhesive dry completely.

6. Place your finished medallion on top of the piece of scrap wood. Position the nail at the top of the washer's center hole. Hammer the nail, making sure to go through all the layers of felt, to create a hole for the needle and necklace cord.

7. Thread the 2 cut ends of necklace cord onto a large-eyed needle. Push the needle through the medallion hole, leaving a 1″ loop of cord hanging out the front. Thread the needle back through the loop and pull it snug.

8. Check that the cord fits easily over your head and the medallion is lying where you want it. Tie a knot about 12¼″ (or desired length) from the top of the finished felt medallion. Cut the extra cording off about ¼″ from the knot.

Holiday Tree Wall Art

Finished Size: 25″ × 64″

For this project, I used circles as my embellishment theme—from wooden buttons to book rings. This project encourages family involvement, and the result can easily become a treasured family heirloom. Feel free to add sentimental findings—perhaps a button from Grandpa's shirt, a sweet ribbon from something special, or Fido's original dog license. It's totally up to you. The main thing is to have fun!

Materials

Burlap: 2 yards (48″ wide)

Quilting-weight cotton: 2 yards

Quilt batting: 2 yards (or twin-size batting)

Brown felt: 1″ × 5″

Wooden dowels, 3–5mm: 1 piece 12″ long, 2 pieces 24″ long

Hardware for dowels: 2 eyelet screws, 1 hook eyelet screw

Spray adhesive

Fabric-marking pen (Always test on a scrap of fabric before using. I recommend using FriXion pens.)

Thread to coordinate with fabric

Embroidery floss and needles (You may need several needles with large and small eyes, depending on the size of your floss and embellishments.)

Pins (with glass heads)

Masking tape

Metal tape measure

Hammer and nail

Assorted embellishments

Optional but Helpful
Rotary cutter, clear Omnigrid ruler, and self-healing cutting mat

Seam gauge

Note: Burlap can be a bit loose and wiggly to work with, so these optional tools make it easier to cut straight lines.

Make It

Cutting

Wash, dry, and press the cotton fabric before you cut it. Do not wash the batting or the burlap.

Burlap: 25″ × 72″

Cotton fabric: 28″ × 64″

Batting: 28″ × 64″ (Make sure you have enough to cover the cotton fabric.)

Brown felt: 1″ × 5″

Make the Triangle Tree

1. Position the cotton quilting fabric on top of the batting, right side up. Begin in the center and carefully pin every 2″–4″.

2. Quilt the 2 layers (fabric side up) on the sewing machine in any way you'd like. I used straight stitches back and forth to create a zigzag pattern.

3. Fold the panel in half, matching up the long sides (batting to batting). Secure with a few pins. Trim off a short end at a 90° angle. This is the bottom.

4. Using a fabric-marking pen, mark the following points necessary to draw a cut line for the triangle tree:

a. With the quilted fabric still folded in half, measure 12″ from the folded side (along the bottom, cut edge) and mark that point.

b. Along the folded edge, make a mark 60″ from the bottom.

c. Extend a tape measure from the 60″ mark to the 12″ mark at the bottom. Secure the tape measure with masking tape and draw a line from mark to mark.

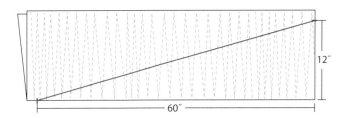

5. Remove the tape measure, add a couple of pins to keep the fabric neatly folded in half, and carefully cut along the line you made in Step 4c. Be sure to cut through all the layers.

6. Unfold the fabric. You now have a nice quilted triangle tree that is 24″ wide at the bottom and 60″ high.

TIP

Use the extra quilted fabric to make ornaments or hang tags!

Make the Burlap Foundation

Note: Use a pressing cloth between your iron and the burlap.

1. Fold the burlap in half (long sides matched up) and trim both of the short ends to a 90° angle. Then cut the burlap so it is 25″ wide and 70″ long.

2. In Step 1, we cut off the stitched selvage edges. Using a straight stitch, sew along both long sides, ⅝″ from the edge, twice to give it an extra-strong hold. Pull some of the burlap strings from each side in order to fray the edge a bit and match the original selvage.

Make the Top Pocket

1. To make the pocket for the top wooden dowel, fold a short end (this will be the top of your wallhanging) over 1″ and press. Fold it over again (in the same direction) 2″ and press again.

2. Pin the hem in place and then use a straight stitch to sew down the fold for the dowel.

Add the Tree, Tree Trunk, and Hem

1. Place the quilted tree fabric side down on a surface protected with newsprint or paper. Following the manufacturer's directions, carefully spray adhesive to the batting side of the tree. (Be sure to do this in a well-ventilated area.)

2. Spread out the burlap panel right side up (the pocket for the dowel will be on the back) on a surface protected with newsprint or paper.

3. On the burlap, find the center point of the top. Just below the stitch line of the pocket, place the top point of the quilted triangle tree. Be sure the bottom of the tree is centered on the burlap. Press firmly to adhere the tree to the burlap.

4. Use a wide zigzag stitch to sew around all 3 sides of the tree to cover the raw edges.

5. Find the center of the bottom of the tree and pin the brown felt vertically, centered on the center mark. Stitch this down with a zigzag stitch around all 4 raw edges.

6. From the bottom of the tree, measure 5″ down and trim the remainder of the burlap away.

7. To make the bottom pocket for the bottom wooden dowel, fold over the bottom edge to the back 1″ and press. Fold it over again 2″ and press again. Pin it in place and stitch the pocket down with a straight stitch.

Add the Wooden Dowels

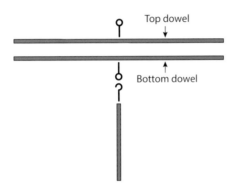

Top dowel

Bottom dowel

1. Find the center point of a 24″ wooden dowel, make a dot, and hammer a nail partway into the dowel (to make it easier to find the spot to screw in the eyelet). Remove the nail. Repeat with the second dowel.

2. Insert the first dowel into the top pocket, making certain to align the nail hole facing up—toward the top of the pocket. Find the center hole you started and screw in the eyelet screw. Screw it in as tight as you can. (To find the hole, insert the eyelet at the center point of the burlap pocket and match it up with the nail hole by feel.)

3. Repeat Step 2 with the bottom pocket. Make sure the nail hole is facing down. Insert the dowel, find the center hole in the wood, and screw in the eyelet screw.

4. Screw the "hook" eyelet into one of the round ends of the 12″ dowel.

Finish It

1. Time to embellish! Lay out the wallhanging right side up. Have some fun organizing and placing your embellishments (washers, buttons, Fido's dog license, etc.) where you think they look best.

2. Take a snapshot for reference (several close-up shots can make it that much easier to place things where you want them). *Or* throw all caution to the wind and just *go for it*! Sometimes this is the most fun and can actually create more interesting results. Stitch your treasures onto the tree.

3. After you have everything sewn in place, you need a sturdy hook—placed high enough on the wall so there is room for the hanging wooden dowel to be hooked onto the bottom eyelet screw.

Uncle Bruce's Glögg

Makes about ½ gallon • **Preparation/cooking time: 55 minutes**

Glögg—pronounced glooog (not glug)—is a hot mulled wine that warms both the body and soul. Uncle Bruce (our family cocktail connoisseur) is often in charge of the *glögg* making at our house during the holidays. And as Unc would say after the first sip, "This will do."

Ingredients

1 bottle red wine

2 cups vodka or brandy

1 cinnamon stick (break into large pieces)

½ teaspoon cardamom seeds

½ orange peel

6–8 cloves

½ cup seedless raisins

½ cup blanched almonds

Extra cinnamon sticks for garnish *(optional)*

Directions

1. Pour the red wine and vodka (or brandy) into a saucepan. Add all the remaining ingredients.

2. Simmer for about 45 minutes. Do not boil.

3. While hot, strain the liquid through cheesecloth or a fine-mesh sieve into *small* mugs or glasses to remove the spices. (Add a few of the strained raisins and almonds back into the mugs, too.)

4. *Optional:* Garnish with a cinnamon stick.

Swedish Tomte Softie

Finished Size: 5″ × 12″

Tomtes are mischievous little spirits in charge of protecting the home and the people who live there. They don't ask for too much, just that we believe in them and offer them a steamy bowl of Christmas porridge with a dab of butter on Christmas Eve.

Materials

Red and white cotton print 1: 1 fat quarter or ¼ yard

Red and white cotton print 2: 1 fat quarter or ¼ yard

Wool-blend felt: 4 squares 6″ × 6″ (1 square each of red, white, pink, and brown)

Muslin or other scrap fabric: 1 fat quarter or 2 pieces 4½″ × 5½″

Polyester filling: 2 ounces

Dry beans: ½ cup

Fabric-marking pen (Always test on a scrap of fabric before using. I recommend using FriXion pens.)

Fine-tip permanent marker

White printer/copier paper, 8½″ × 11″: 6 sheets (or 1 sheet 14″ × 17″ tracing paper)

Basting glue (I recommend Roxanne Glue-Baste-It.)

Coordinating all-purpose sewing thread

Hand-sewing needle and threader

Make It

You can enlarge or reduce the pattern pieces to make a tomte in a different size.

Use an ⅛" seam allowance unless otherwise noted.

Make the Pieces

1. Using a fine-tip marker and paper, trace the tomte pattern pieces A, B, C, D, E, F, G, H, I, and J (pullout page P1) and then cut out each shape.

2. Using a fabric-marking pen and the pattern pieces cut in Step 1, trace the shapes onto the fabric and felt as indicated on the pattern. Don't forget to add the alignment marks noted on the patterns.

3. Cut out all the felt and fabric shapes.

Make the Arms and Legs

1. Add dabs of glue to the straight edge of an arm about ⅛" from the end. Place the squared end of a hand over the arm, overlapping the pieces ¼". Flip over. Add glue dots to the surface of the hand. Place a second felt hand on top of the glued hand to make a hand and arm sandwich. Repeat for the other hand and arm.

2. Repeat the process described in Step 1 with the feet and legs. You should end up with 2 leg and feet sandwiches. Allow the glue to dry before moving to Step 3.

3. Zigzag stitch around each hand and foot, using either matching or contrasting thread. Using a straight stitch, sew up each side of the arms and legs to give them a nice finished look.

Make the Body

1. Using basting glue, baste the white felt beard to the front body panel. Match up the top straight edge of the beard to the beard alignment marks on the body. Then sew a straight stitch around the edges of the beard, about 1/16″ from the edge.

2. Place the arms and legs onto the front of the body panel and hand baste them in place with a few running stitches (see Tomte placement diagram, at right).

3. Place the back body panel on top of the front body panel, right sides together.

4. Stitch along each of the *long sides*, leaving a 3″ opening on a side near the top. *Make sure you do not sew the bottom side yet.* Without cutting into your stitches, cut the top point of the seam allowance off to reduce bulk.

5. Leave the body as is—inside out. With right sides together, match the alignment marks on the oval bottom panel to the side seams of the body. Pin around the bottom, easing bulk.

6. Sew, moving slowly and stopping when necessary to adjust for the curve.

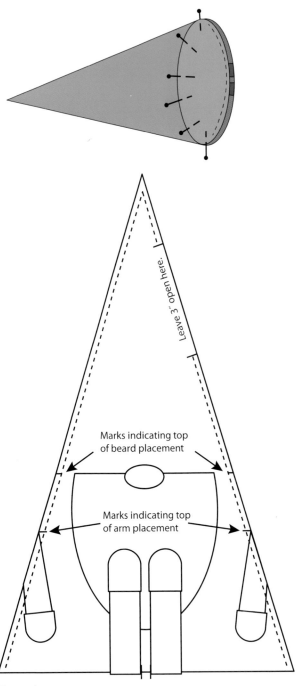

Leave 3″ open here.

Marks indicating top of beard placement

Marks indicating top of arm placement

Tomte placement

7. Pull the body back through the open area on the side so that it is right side out.

8. To make the beanbag, sew the 2 muslin ovals together, leaving a 1½″ opening—no need to turn the bag inside out. Fill the bag with beans and sew the opening closed.

9. Insert the beanbag into the body through the opening and smooth it out so it lies flat at the bottom of the body.

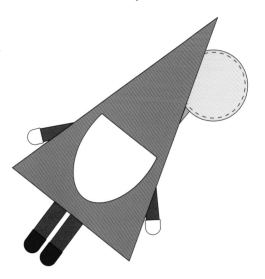

10. Stuff the body with polyester filling. Use a chopstick, an awl, or even scissors (carefully) to get the stuffing into the tight point at the top. Fill the body until it's firm and well rounded, then hand stitch the opening closed. Note: The hat will cover your hand stitching.

Make the Hat and Finish

1. Fold the hat panel in half with right sides together, matching up the long straight edges. Sew the seam, clip the point (without cutting the stitches), and turn the hat right side out.

2. Fold the curved edge of the hat under ⅛″ and finger-press. Using a straight stitch, sew the edge down ¹⁄₁₆″ from the edge. Press.

3. Pull the hat over the top of the body as far as it will go. Stitch a few tack stitches on the sides and back of the hat to attach it to the body so that it stays in place.

4. Glue the felt nose into position—it should overlap the hat's brim (see the placement diagram, page 27)—and hand stitch it in place with a whipstitch (see Stitches, page 109).

5. Carefully iron out any wrinkles using a light steam setting.

MAKE TOMTE HAPPY

Instead of leaving cookies and milk out for Santa, a bowl of Christmas porridge is served to Tomte—a small, mischievous elf. He has become known as the Swedish Santa (influenced over time by the version of Santa we are most familiar with today). Although he is known to travel in a sleigh pulled by reindeer and deliver gifts to children, his *real* job (unlike Santa's) is to oversee a home's safety and prosperity. If he does not feel appreciated, however, he may start playing tricks on you—hence, the importance of making sure Tomte is presented with a lovely bowl of porridge with a generous helping of butter on Christmas Eve!

Swedish Christmas Porridge

Makes 6–8 servings
Total preparation/cooking time: 45 minutes to 1 hour

Serve this porridge in small bowls on Christmas Eve. Be sure to set aside a small cup for your tomte, and put some butter on it to keep him happy!

Ingredients

1 cup white rice (Do *not* use "instant" or quick-cook rice.)

4 cups milk

2 cups water

½ teaspoon salt

2 tablespoons sugar

2 tablespoons butter

1 blanched almond

Garnishes: cinnamon sugar, butter, milk, or fruit jam or lingonberry sauce (page 41) to taste

Directions

1. Rinse and drain the rice. Put all the ingredients, except the almond, into a saucepan. Bring the rice mixture to a boil, stirring continuously to prevent sticking.

2. Reduce the heat and bring the mixture down to a simmer. Cover the saucepan and let the rice simmer for 30–45 minutes or until thick and creamy.

3. Add a single blanched almond to the mixture before serving. Whoever finds the almond gets the "almond gift"—which can be as simple or elaborate as you choose!

4. Serve the porridge. Be sure to have the garnishes available at the table.

Bread Warmer Tea Towel

Finished Size: 20″ × 28″

Bread has been an essential staple of everyday life in most societies for centuries. Scandinavia is no different. It seems everywhere you go, there's a loaf of bread sitting on a wooden cutting board, wrapped in a tea towel, anticipating that another slice will be cut and enjoyed.

Materials

Linen or linen/cotton-blend fabric: ⅔ yard for towel

Coordinating appliqué fabric (linen, linen/cotton blend, or quilting cotton): 1 fat quarter or ¼ yard (Use a single fabric or a combination. You will have extra fabric left over.)

Iron-on adhesive: ¼ yard (I used Heat*n*Bond Feather Lite.)

All-purpose sewing thread to coordinate with towel fabric

All-purpose sewing thread to coordinate with appliqué fabric(s)

Contrasting embroidery floss: 1 skein

Fine-tip permanent marker

Fabric-marking pen (Always test on a scrap of fabric before using. I recommend using FriXion pens.)

Optional but Helpful

Rotary cutter, clear Omnigrid ruler, and self-healing cutting mat

Seam gauge

¼″ double-fold bias tape: 6″, to hang towel on hook

Cutting

Wash, dry, and press the fabric before you cut it.

Tea towel fabric: 21″ × 29″

Appliqué fabric: 5″ × 14″

Linen Fabric Care

Linen fabric (made from flax) has been used to make clothing and home wares for thousands of years—long before we had dry cleaners available. One of the best features of linen is that it gets softer and more absorbent the more it is used and washed, so go ahead—wash your linen! Hand or machine wash in cold or lukewarm water using mild soap and a gentle cycle. You can machine dry linen at a cool temperature and remove the fabric while it is still damp (or lay it flat to air dry). While the linen is still damp, press out the wrinkles using a steam iron on a medium to high setting. It's best to iron linen on the wrong side of the fabric, especially dark colors. If you want to keep your linen looking super crisp, dry cleaning is the way to go. It's just nice to know we have options.

Make It

Use a ¼" seam allowance unless otherwise noted.

1. Use a fine-tip marker to trace the rectangle and oval appliqué pattern pieces 1–5 (pullout page P1) onto the paper side of the iron-on adhesive. Cut the paper rectangle out (don't cut out the circles within it just yet).

2. Place the appliqué fabric right side down on the ironing board. Place the iron-on adhesive on top, paper side up. Make sure your fabric is slightly larger than the paper template. Use a pressing cloth to avoid getting adhesive and ink on your iron. Following the manufacturer's instructions, press the adhesive onto the fabric.

3. Cut out each of the appliqué shapes, including the inner ovals.

4. Remove the paper backing and place the appliqués adhesive side down on the front side of the tea towel fabric. The center of the circle appliqués should be placed 5½" from the right edge and a little more than ½" from the bottom. (See the diagram, page 33.) Press the appliqués in place.

5. Using thread that matches the appliqués, zigzag stitch the appliqués onto the tea towel. Refer to Finishing Zigzag Stitches (page 39) if needed.

> **TIP**
> Make sure you've got the stitch settings for your machine just right by testing them on scrap fabric before starting the actual project.

Finish It

1. Finish the raw edges of the tea towel by folding each raw edge over, wrong sides together, ¼″ and pressing. Fold each side over another ¼″ and press again, pinning as you go. Use a straight stitch to topstitch the folded edges down. (If you are adding the strip of bias tape to the top corner, trim the bias tape to 4″, cutting the edges at a 45° angle as shown in the diagram below, and tuck it into the seam allowance fold before sewing.)

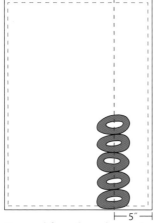 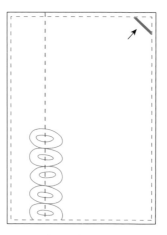

Tea towel front shown hemmed with top stitching

Tea towel back shown hemmed with top stitching. Bias tape placed under seam allowance

2. Gently mark a dotted line up the center of the appliqué circles using a ruler and fabric-marking pen. (The line should be about 5″ from the right side of the tea towel.)

3. Tie a knot at the end of a thick piece of embroidery floss, leaving a 3″ tail. Come up from the back of the tea towel and embroider a running stitch up the line made in Step 2. Refer to Stitches (page 109) as needed.

4. On the back of the towel, tie a knot at the end of the floss. Similar to the way the zigzag stitches were finished (see Finishing Zigzag Stitches, page 39), you can thread the loose ends of embroidery floss and pull them into the hidden fold of the edge seam. Trim the ends close to the fabric and you'll never know they are there!

Make Bias Tape

It's easy to make your own bias tape with the fabric you're using for your project:

1. Cut a strip of fabric 1″ × 6″ on the bias. Fold it in half, wrong sides together, so that the long sides match up. Press.

2. Open the fold so that the wrong side of the fabric faces up; then fold each of the long sides in so the raw edges align with the center crease. Press these new folds.

3. Fold the strip in half again lengthwise along the center fold and press. Use a straight stitch to stitch it together. You now have double-fold ¼″ bias tape!

Grandma Ragnhild's Limpa (Rye Bread)

Makes 2 large (9″ × 5″) loaves • Preparation time: about 6 hours

My cousin (in-law) Tim, our family baker extraordinaire, grew up baking this recipe for *limpa* (Swedish rye bread) with his grandma Ragnhild. Thanks to Tim, we always have *limpa* during the holidays, but it is delicious any time of year! I hope you enjoy it as much as our family does!

Ingredients

SPONGE

1 packet yeast (2¼ teaspoons)

2 cups lukewarm water, divided

2 teaspoons sugar

1½ cups unbleached all-purpose flour

DOUGH

1¼ cups dark rye flour

3 or 4 cups unbleached all-purpose flour

½ cup sugar

1 tablespoon salt

2 tablespoons vegetable oil

6 tablespoons molasses

¼ cup wheat germ

2¼ teaspoons ground anise seed

2¼ teaspoons ground fennel seed

"Battre grov kaka an ingen smaka."

Better coarse bread than none at all. In other words …
be thankful for what you have.

Directions

1. To begin the sponge, pour the sugar and 1 cup of water into a large bowl. Sprinkle the yeast over the water and stir until it dissolves.

2. After bubbles form, add the remaining cup of water and the 1½ cups of all-purpose flour. Mix together to form a spongy dough. Cover the bowl with a clean dish towel or plastic wrap and let the sponge rest for 1 hour.

3. Stir the remaining ingredients into the sponge to make a fairly stiff and somewhat sticky dough. (When adding all-purpose flour, add 3 cups and, if needed, add more ½ cup at a time until the dough is as described above.) Turn out the dough onto a floured board and knead it for as long as you have the strength and interest. Add flour as needed to keep the dough from sticking to the board.

4. Form the dough into a ball and place it into a large greased bowl. Turn the ball over so the greased side is up. Cover it with a dish towel or plastic wrap and let it rise in a warm place until it has doubled in bulk. Punch down the dough in the bowl, cover, and let it rise again until it doubles in bulk.

5. Punch the dough down once more and then divide it into 2 parts. Shape the 2 parts into loaves. Place the dough in greased loaf pans, cover the loaves with a towel or plastic wrap, and let them rise in a warm place until they are doubled in size. The loaves are ready to bake when you can touch the dough lightly and a slight indent remains.

6. Bake at 325° F for about 45 minutes (or until the loaves are nicely browned) on a rack positioned in the bottom third of the oven. Remove the loaves from the oven and let them cool in the pans for 10 minutes; then turn them out onto a baking rack to cool completely.

Linen Table Runner

Finished Size: 13″ × 48″

This appliquéd table runner, which coordinates with the Bread Warmer Tea Towel (page 30), will be a fresh addition to any urban kitchen.

Materials

Panel A: ½ yard linen or linen/cotton-blend fabric

Panels B and C: 1 fat quarter or ¼ yard contrasting linen or linen/cotton-blend fabric

Coordinating appliqué fabric: 1 fat quarter or ¼ yard (Use 1 fabric or a combination. You will have extra fabric left over.)

Iron-on adhesive: ½ yard (I used Heat*n*Bond Feather Lite.)

Fine-tip permanent marker

Fabric-marking pen (Always test on a scrap of fabric before using. I recommend using FriXion pens.)

All-purpose sewing thread to coordinate with panel A fabric

All-purpose sewing thread(s) to coordinate with contrasting fabric(s)

Contrasting embroidery floss: 1 skein

Embroidery floss threader and needle

Optional but Helpful

Rotary cutter, clear Omnigrid ruler, and self-healing cutting mat

Seam gauge

Cutting

Wash, dry, and press the fabric before you cut it. (See Linen Fabric Care, page 32.)

Panel A: 14″ × 31½″

Panel B: 1¾″ × 14″

Panel C: 14″ × 16¾″

Appliqué fabric: 10″ × 14″

Make It

Use a ¼" seam allowance unless otherwise noted.

Piece It

> **TIP**
>
> Make sure you've got the stitch settings for your machine just right by testing them on scrap fabric before starting on the actual project.

Panels A, B, and C placement

1. Following the placement diagram above, pin the panels together with right sides facing. Sew the 3 panels together using a straight stitch. Press the seams open.

2. Zigzag stitch over the raw edge of each back seam. Your top and bobbin thread should match the fabric you are sewing on.

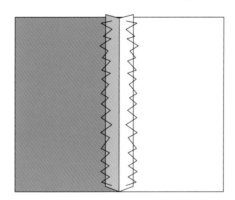

Appliqué It

1. Use a permanent marker to trace the circular appliqué pattern (pullout page P1) onto the paper side of the iron-on adhesive and then cut out the paper rectangle (do not cut out the circles within it just yet). No need to draw the dashed line.

2. Repeat Step 1 to create a second set of appliqués. Draw the dashed line running through the circles on this set.

3. Place the appliqué fabrics right side down on the ironing board. Place both iron-on adhesive sheets on top, paper side up. Make sure the fabric is slightly larger than the paper template. Use a pressing cloth to avoid getting adhesive and ink on your iron. Following the manufacturer's instructions, press the adhesive onto the fabric.

4. Cut out the first set of appliqué shapes, including the inner circles.

5. For the second set of appliqués, cut along the dashed line to remove the side without the numbers. Then cut the curves of the circles.

6. Referring to the placement diagram, place the panel A and panel C appliqués adhesive side down on the front side of the table runner. Be sure the panel A appliqués are aligned with the raw edge of the panel fabric and the panel C appliqués begin about ½" from the short end. Press the appliqués into place like you did in Step 3.

7. Use a zigzag stitch with thread to match the appliqué fabric to stitch the appliqués onto the table runner.

Finishing Zigzag Stitches

Thread any loose ends of thread on your hand-sewing needle and bring them to the back side. Tie a knot and then run the thread ends through several of the zigzag stitches on the back.

Finish It

1. Finish the raw edges of the runner by folding each raw edge under, wrong sides together, ¼" and pressing. Fold each side under another ¼" and press again, pinning as you go. Use a straight stitch to topstitch the folded edges down.

2. Gently make a dotted line up the center of the appliqué circles on panel C using a ruler and fabric-marking pen.

3. Tie a knot at the end of a 45" length of embroidery floss (do not separate the strands; use it as it comes off the skein), leaving a 3" tail. Come up from the back of the runner and embroider a running stitch up the line made in Step 2. Refer to Stitches (page 109) as needed.

4. On the back of the runner, tie a knot at the end of the floss. Similar to the way the zigzag stitches were finished, you can thread the loose ends of embroidery floss and pull them into the hidden fold of the edge seam. Trim the ends close to the fabric and you'll never know they're there!

Grandma Vera's Swedish Meatballs

Serves 4–6 • Preparation/cooking time: 1 hour

There are about as many versions of Swedish meatballs as there are Swedes, but according to my grandma Vera, they're not Swedish meatballs if they are bigger than 1″ across. Make them small and make them many!

Ingredients

¾ pound ground sirloin beef

¼ pound ground pork

¼ cup finely chopped onion

2 tablespoons butter, separated

3 slices dried bread (with crusts removed)

¼ cup milk

1 egg

1 teaspoon salt

1 teaspoon Worcestershire sauce

½ teaspoon pepper

¼ teaspoon nutmeg

½ teaspoon ground cardamom

Fresh parsley

Directions

1. Sauté the onion in 1 tablespoon butter until soft and translucent. Cool slightly.

2. Pulverize the bread in a blender or food processor, creating fine bread crumbs. Set aside.

3. Combine the sautéed onions, egg, milk, and spices until smooth, using a mixer, blender, or food processor. Remove to a mixing bowl.

4. Add the ground beef, pork, and bread crumbs. Cover the mixture and refrigerate for an hour.

5. Roll the mixture into 1″ balls (Swedish meatballs are quite small). Brown the meatballs in a pan with 1 tablespoon butter until they are cooked. Sprinkle with fresh parsley. Serve.

Swedish meatballs are traditionally served with boiled (or mashed) potatoes, seasonal vegetables, and lingonberry sauce (page 41).

Lingonberry Sauce

Makes 2½ cups • Preparation/cooking time: ½ hour

Lingonberry sauce is a staple in Scandinavian kitchens all year round. It is served as a condiment to savory meat dishes or as a tangy sweet dessert topping.

Ingredients

3½ cups lingonberries

1 cup water

1 cup sugar

Directions

1. Bring the water and sugar to a boil in a heavy-bottomed pan.

2. Add in the lingonberries and simmer uncovered for about 20 minutes.

3. Allow the sauce to cool. Store in the refrigerator or freeze in half-pint containers. Sauce will thicken when chilled.

Felt Cup Warmer

Finished Size: 3¼″ × 16″

This no-sew project makes it easy to warm hands and hearts—just by filling the felt-wrapped mugs with treats for family and friends.

Materials

White mug with straight sides (Mine was 11 ounces and 3″ across.)

Felt: 2 sheets 12″ × 18″ in different colors (You will have enough left over to make 2 additional cup warmers.)

2 buttons, ½″

Fabric-marking pen (Always test on a scrap of fabric before using. I recommend using FriXion pens.)

White printer/copier paper: 2 sheets 8½″ × 11″

Spray adhesive

Embroidery floss: 1 skein (I used white.)

Cutting

Felt color 1: 4″ × 10¼″ (for pattern A)

Felt color 2: 4″ × 18″ (for pattern B)

> **TIP**
>
> If your mug is larger than 3″ in diameter, cut pattern pieces A and B where indicated and tape a piece of paper wide enough to accommodate your mug. You may need a larger piece of felt to accommodate the larger pattern.

Make It

1. Trace pattern piece A (pullout page P2) onto a sheet of paper. Cut out the rectangle and the heart within the rectangle.

2. Place them on top of felt color 1 (the 4″ × 10¼″ piece of felt), aligning the edges. Trace the heart shape onto the felt with a fabric-marking pen. Cut out the heart.

3. Cut 1 piece of paper 8½″ × 11″ in half lengthwise and tape the 2 pieces together at the short end. Trace pattern piece B (pullout page P2) onto this sheet of paper. Cut out the shape, including the inner heart shape.

4. Place felt color 1 on a surface protected with newsprint or paper. Following the manufacturer's directions, carefully spray adhesive to a side of the felt. (Be sure to do this in a well-ventilated area.) Carefully lay the sticky side of the felt on top of

felt color 2, aligning a short side (see the diagram below), to adhere the pieces together.

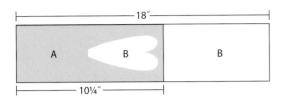

5. Align the open heart of pattern piece B to the open heart of felt piece 1. Trace the perimeter of pattern piece B with a fabric-marking pen. (If needed, you can put a couple of pieces of rolled tape between the template and the felt to hold it in place.) Transfer the markings for the button and buttonhole placement. The bottom button is decorative—no buttonhole.

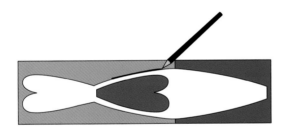

6. Remove the paper template and cut out the final felt shape along the traced lines you made in Step 5.

7. Slip the small end of the felt through the handle of your mug and tape it down to secure it. Wrap the felt around the mug and tuck the heart end through the cup handle.

8. Stick a pin through the center of the buttonhole cut line. With a pen, mark a dot

where the pin goes through to the second layer. This is the placement for the top button.

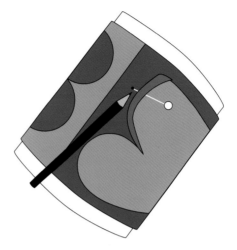

9. Remove the felt from the mug and sew on the buttons with embroidery floss. The top button should be sewn on the dot marked in Step 8.

10. Put the small straight edge of the felt through the mug's handle again and tape to secure it. Wrap the felt around the mug and tuck the heart end through the handle. Pull it snug, so the felt lies flat around the entire mug.

11. The top right curve of the heart should be on top of the top button. Check that the cut line looks and feels like it is in line with the button (redraw the line if needed). Carefully cut the buttonhole and pull the button through the hole.

12. Remove the tape from under the handle area. Remove any visible fabric pen marks according to the manufacturer's instructions.

Appliquéd Winter Quilt

Finished Size: 80″ × 88″

In the cold winter months, nothing is better than having a bright quilt to ward off the dark season's blues. A bit unconventional in approach, this quilt features three long quilted panels pieced together. No longarm or fancy quilting equipment required.

Materials

Coordinating cotton or linen/cotton-blend fabric in 5 colors:

Panel A: Cream, 3 yards* 45″ wide

Panel B: Cream, 3 yards, or 1½ yards if pieced at the center (This is the background fabric for the appliqués.)*

Panel C: Pink, 1 yard

Panel D: Gray, 1¾ yards

Panel E: Orange, ⅜ yard

Patterned fabric for backing: 6 yards, at least 42″ wide

Muslin: 6 yards (60″ wide)

Low-loft batting, king size

Iron-on adhesive: 2 yards (I used HeatnBond Feather Lite.)

Coordinating thread

Measuring tape and ruler

Fabric-marking pen (Always test on a scrap of fabric before using. I recommend using FriXion pens.)

Rotary cutter and self-healing cutting mat

T square (*optional*)

* Note: If you choose to use 60″-wide fabric, purchase 3 yards only to use for both panels A and B.

Cutting

Wash, dry, and press the cotton fabric before you cut it. Trim off the selvages.

Panel A: 43″ × 93″

Panel B: 16″ × 93″

Panel C: 25″ × 28″

Panel D: 28″ × 58″

Panel E: 12″ × 28″

Backing: Cut the fabric into 2 sections, each 3 yards long.

60″-wide muslin: Cut 1 section 51″ × 3 yards, 1 section 24″ × 3 yards, and 1 section 34″ × 3 yards.

Batting: Cut 1 rectangle 51″ × 93″, 1 rectangle 24″ × 93″, and 1 rectangle 34″ × 93″.

Appliqué fabrics: Cut leftover fabric from panels C, D, E, and patterned backing fabric into 18″ × 25″ rectangles.

Make It

Use a ½" seam allowance unless otherwise noted.

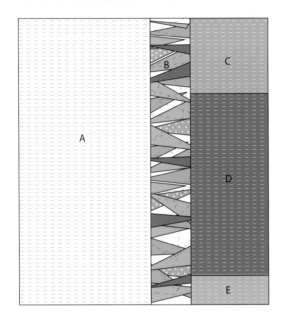

Make the Back Panel

1. Remove the selvages from the backing fabric pieces. Sew, right sides together, along a long edge. Press the back seam open. Flip the backing fabric over (so it's right side up) and topstitch ¼" along each side of the original seam for a nice finished look.

2. Trim the back to measure 81" × 89". Set the extra backing fabric aside to use for the front appliqué.

Make Appliquéd Panel B

1. Apply iron-on adhesive to the back of the appliqué fabrics. Place the appliqué fabric right side down on the ironing board. Place the iron-on adhesive on top, paper side up. Make sure your fabric is slightly larger than the adhesive. Use a pressing cloth to avoid getting adhesive on your iron.

2. Cut random triangular shapes across the 18" width, measuring about 2" to 2½" at the base and about ½" to 1" at the top. You don't have to be precise here—loose, random cuts give this project its character.

3. Cut 12 triangles from each of the solid colors and 6 triangles from the patterned (backing) fabric.

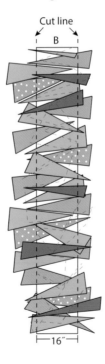

4. Lay out the background fabric for panel B right side up. Arrange the appliqué pieces, adhesive side down, across the background fabric in a wonky, crooked fashion, layering random colors and shapes.

5. Trim any appliqué fabric that extends beyond the sides of the background fabric and use a pressing cloth to avoid getting any adhesive on your ironing surface. Press all the strips in place.

6. When the appliqués are in place, square up the panel so it measures 16″ × 89″.

Piece Panels C, D, and E Together

1. Match panels C and D, right sides together, along a 28″ side. Sew them together.

2. Match a 28″ side of panel E to the bottom of panel D, right sides together. Sew them together. Press all the seams open.

3. Square up this color-blocked panel so that it measures 25″ × 93″.

Quilt Panel A

1. Make sure the muslin, batting, and fabric panel are pressed. With a fabric-marking pen, draw light parallel lines 1½″ apart across the width of the panel on the front side. If you are using a T square, chances are good it is 1½″ wide, which makes marking really easy.

2. Layer the muslin, batting, and panel A fabric right side up. The batting and muslin should extend past the top panel fabric by 3″–4″ on each side. Carefully pin together; then sew along the lines you drew with a straight stitch. (You can use a walking foot to help keep the layers together.)

3. Remove the fabric pen marks, trim off the excess batting and muslin, and square the panel up so that it measures 43″ × 89″.

Quilt Panel B

1. Smooth out the muslin, batting, and appliquéd panel. (Press flat if needed.) The batting and muslin should extend past the panel fabric. Carefully pin together.

2. Use matching thread (or contrasting, if you prefer) to stitch the appliqués and quilt at the same time. You can use a straight stitch, zigzag stitch, or both. Start at the top and stitch until all the appliqués are secured. This is meant to be random and loose, so just go for it! This method of stitching down the appliqués creates a unique zigzaggy pattern (no 2 quilts will ever be the same)!

3. Trim off the excess batting and muslin and square the panel up again so that it measures 15″ × 89″.

Quilt Panel C
(with D and E Pieced)

1. Make sure the muslin, batting, and fabric panel are pressed. With a fabric-marking pen, draw light parallel lines 1½″ apart across the width of the panel on the front side, just like you did in Quilt Panel A, Step 1 (page 49).

2. Layer the muslin, batting, and panel C fabric right side up. The batting and muslin should extend past the top panel fabric by several inches on each side. Carefully pin together; then sew along the lines you drew with a straight stitch.

3. Remove the pen marks, trim off the excess batting and muslin, and square the panel up so that it measures 25″ × 89″.

Finish It

1. Pin panels A and B together, with right sides facing. Take note of the top of the panels so that panel B is to the right of panel A when opened. Sew together using a ½″ seam allowance.

2. Press the seam on the back open. Flip the quilt right side up and topstitch the seam allowances open, stitching ¼″ from each side of the seam you just made.

3. Repeat Steps 1 and 2 to attach the last panel.

4. Square everything up once more to roughly 81″ × 89″. I say roughly, because during all the squaring up, sometimes that figure gets altered a bit. So no worries if it's off a smidge!

5. Lay out the backing fabric and place the finished quilt top on top, right sides together. Smooth everything out, square it up again if necessary, and carefully pin it all together.

6. Stitch around all 4 sides, leaving a 12″–15″ open gap along a side.

7. Being careful not to cut into the stitching, trim off the corners and turn the quilt right side out. For an extra nice flat-finished edge, stitch around the entire perimeter of the quilt ¼″ from the outer edge, then again about ½″ from the edge.

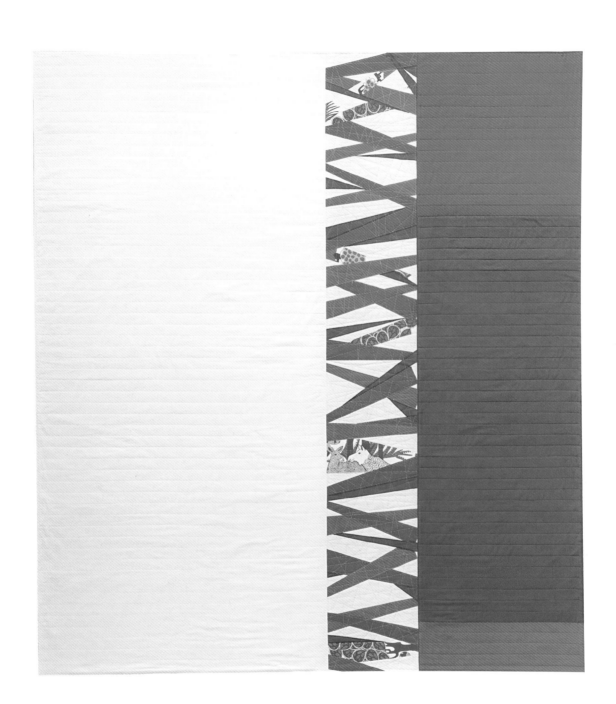

Drafty Door Decor

Finished Size: Approximately 6″ × 45″

This simple reverse-appliqué project adds a bit of warmth and modern style to any drafty door.

Materials

Wool or wool-blend felt: 1 yard each of 2 different colors

Paper-backed iron-on adhesive: 1 yard (I used Heat*n*Bond Feather Lite.)

Fabric-marking pen (Always test on a scrap of fabric before using. I recommend using FriXion pens.)

Fine-tip permanent marker

Sharp-pointed scissors to cut felt

Coordinating thread

Long ruler or measuring tape

Polyester stuffing: 12 ounces

Copy/printer paper: 2 sheets 8½″ × 11″

Optional but Helpful

Rotary cutter, clear Omnigrid ruler, and self-healing cutting mat

Embroidery floss

Embroidery needle and threader

Buttons or other embellishments

Cutting

Felt color 1: Cut 1 rectangle 12½″ × 30″ and 1 rectangle 12½″ × 15″.

Felt color 2: Cut 1 rectangle 12½″ × 30″ and 1 rectangle 12½″ × 15″.

Paper-backed iron-on adhesive: Cut 2 rectangles 6″ × 22″. (You'll have 2 sections that will be placed side by side to make a single adhesive area.)

Make It

1. Overlap the short sides of a 12½″ × 30″ rectangle of color 1 with a 12½″ × 15″ rectangle of color 2 by ¼″. Pin together and stitch together with a zigzag stitch.

2. Repeat Step 1 with the remaining 12½″ × 15″ rectangle of color 1 and 12½″ × 30″ rectangle of color 2.

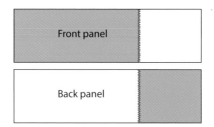

"Uff da!"

An expression of surprise
or mild disappointment,
sort of like "Yikes!" or "Oh, shoot!"

3. Lay the front panel right side down on your ironing board. Place the strips of paper-backed iron-on adhesive, paper side up, on the top half of the back of the felt panel and press in place. It's always good to use a pressing cloth between your iron and any adhesive material (just to make sure you don't get any adhesive on the iron). Let the panel cool; then remove the paper.

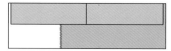

Place paper-backed adhesive strips on wrong side of front panel.

4. Tape the short sides of the copy/printer paper together, creating a long 8½″ × 22″ piece. Trace the pattern (pullout page P2) with a permanent marker, including the rectangle around the teardrops; then cut out the rectangle and teardrop centers.

5. Place the paper template you made in Step 4 on the right side of the pieced felt panel with the adhesive. Align the top edge of the pattern with the top cut edge of the felt. Center the third drop (noted on the pattern) on the zigzag stitched seam. With a fabric pen, trace the teardrop shapes onto the felt, moving the template left and right to complete the design.

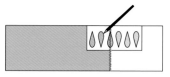

6. Cut out each of the teardrop shapes from the felt.

7. Lay the felt panel with all the shapes cut out over the second felt panel, adhesive side down, and pin the panels together. You should be able to see the opposing colors through the cut-out teardrops.

8. Press the top layer of felt onto the bottom layer of felt. Stitch around each of the appliqué shapes. (I chose a zigzag stitch and matching thread colors, but use contrasting colors if you prefer. Be as creative as you want—there are no rules.)

9. Trim any of the outer edges where the felt may have shifted; then add any embellishments you'd like, such as buttons or embroidery details. I kept mine super simple, with no embellishments.

10. Fold the felt lengthwise, wrong sides together, and pin together. Use a straight stitch and a ¼″ seam allowance to sew around the perimeter, including the folded edge. Leave 6″ open for stuffing.

Leave 6″ open for stuffing.

11. Add the stuffing. Once you have it stuffed as much as you'd like, stitch up the 6″ opening to close it off.

Midsummer

Midsummer (or *Midsommar*) is the longest day of the year. Midsummer's Eve is celebrated the first Friday after the summer solstice with as much zest as the winter holiday season (perhaps even more!). In Sweden, it's right up there with Christmas.

Although the main Midsummer celebrations land on a particular day, it's a great excuse to take (at the very least) an extra-long weekend or extended holiday. There is a mass exodus from anything that resembles work—most businesses are totally shut down. My mom and I happened to arrive in Stockholm on Midsummer's Eve on a recent trip and, no kidding, there was *nothing* open. We weren't sure anyone would be at the front desk to check us into our hotel room (a bit of an exaggeration, but not by too much). It's such a big deal in Sweden that there is serious talk of changing Midsummer's Eve into the National Day of Sweden.

Midsummer is a magical time of year when anything seems possible. It's all about enjoying the long days with friends and family and taking that long-awaited warm-weather holiday. Do something you love to do—especially some summer stitching—and enjoy!

Skirt Apron

Finished Size: Varies
(size will be determined by your measurements—
example in photo approximately 44″ × 20″)

Many traditional Scandinavian costumes incorporate a *dress apron*. For a modern twist on this tradition, throw this sheer apron over a bright-colored skirt and serve up some cool Midsummer cocktails to celebrate the season!

Materials

White voile, 100% cotton, 54″–56″ wide: 1 yard

All-purpose white sewing thread

White gift-wrapping tissue paper, 2–3 sheets

Kraft paper roll (Paper grocery bags work, too!)

Fabric-marking pen (Always test on a scrap of fabric before using. I recommend FriXion pens.)

Single-fold bias tape, ⅞″ wide: 3 yards (I used white.)

NOTE

The materials listed are based on the apron I made—so just be aware that the measurements and materials might be adjusted somewhat based on your measurements.

Bjudning = Party

No Midsummer party would be worth a hill of beans without a lot of great food and drink to accompany a lot of great music and dancing.

Make It

Make the Paper Template

1. Measure your waist. Then measure from your waist down to determine how long you want your apron to be. Add ½″ to that length to get the final measurement.

My example: 30″ × 20½″

2. On the kraft paper, draw a rectangle according to your measurements. (Tape several pieces of paper together if necessary.) Divide the width into 6 equal parts. Draw dashed lines on the paper template to indicate these dividing lines.

I divided 30″ by 6, ending up with 6 sections 5″ wide.

3. Cut out the rectangle from the kraft paper. Cut along the dashed dividing lines, *leaving the paper attached* at the top by about 1″.

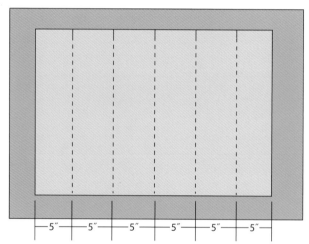

Do not cut the last 1″ at the top.

4. Get a fresh piece of kraft paper that's a bit larger than the first. Take the template you cut out and spread the divided sections 3″ apart at the bottom. Tape the sections securely to the second layer of paper.

5. Lay the voile fabric over the paper template and trace the outline with a fabric-marking pen. Cut out the fabric along the traced line. It will be wider at the bottom than the top.

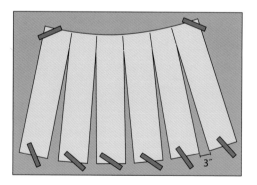

Make the Flower Appliqué

1. Get out a fresh sheet of kraft paper and an 8″-diameter salad plate. Use the plate to trace 5 connecting half-circles to make a big 5-petal flower. Your flower will be about 18″ in diameter.

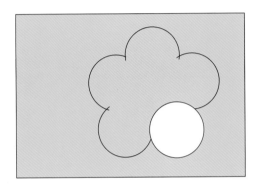

2. Lay the appliqué fabric on top of the paper flower and trace the flower onto the fabric. Cut out the fabric flower.

3. Take a roughly 7″-diameter dish and trace a circle onto a separate piece of fabric; cut it out. Cut off the top quarter of the circle, fold the edge over ¼″ twice, and topstitch. This will be the top of the flower pocket.

4. Lay out a smoothed-flat piece of tissue paper under the apron panel. (Note: The tissue paper can be pressed flat with the steam setting off, if necessary). Place the flower appliqué where you'd like it to be on the apron, and then place the center pocket you made in Step 3 on top of the flower. Make sure there's tissue behind the *entire* flower appliqué area. Pin all the layers together with the appliqué as flat as possible. It is OK if the flower runs off the apron a bit—it's meant to be a BIG flower.

> **TIP**
>
> The tissue paper acts as a nonslippery base under the very lightweight sheer fabric, making sewing easier. It helps keep the fabric flat and prevents puckering.

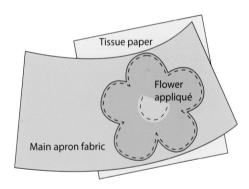

Tissue paper

Flower appliqué

Main apron fabric

5. Using a straight stitch, sew around the perimeter of the flower and the rounded area of the center pocket, ¼″ from the edge. When finished, carefully remove the tissue from the stitching on the back.

MIDSUMMER TIDBITS

Midsummer is when the sailboats begin dotting the waterways and bonfires light up the beaches. New potatoes tossed with fresh herbs, meatballs, pickled herring, cheese with flat bread, beer, and a bottomless glass of spiced schnapps accompanied by *snapsvisor* (traditional drinking songs) abound. Having a midnight meal is traditional, too—and an excuse to have a bit more schnapps, a few more new potatoes, and herring along with some fresh berries (of any kind really, but strawberries, lingonberries, and cloudberries are common—topped with fresh cream, of course).

Finish It

1. Finish the side seams and hem by folding the raw edge over ¼″ twice and topstitching with a straight stitch.

2. Iron the bias tape. Find the center point and line it up with the center point of the top of the apron. Sandwich the raw edge at the top of the apron inside the folded bias tape. Pin it securely; then sew a straight stitch along the entire length of the bias tape to close it off and attach it to the top of the skirt.

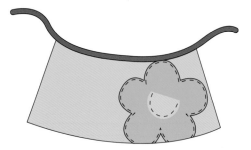

That's it! You've now got a super-sassy Midsummer apron skirt to flirt up your next gathering.

Lingonberry Sorbet

Makes 3 pints (6 cups) • Preparation/cooking time: about 1 hour

Lingonberry sorbet, both tangy and sweet, is the perfect way to top off a warm Midsummer meal.

Ingredients

4 cups lingonberries (if frozen, thaw, strain thawed berries, and see Tip, below.)

1 cup extra-fine sugar

⅓ cup orange juice

⅓ cup lemon juice

2 tablespoons aquavit (or vodka)

TIP

Reserve the liquid from the berry-straining process and add it to orange juice or lemonade for another Midsummer treat!

Directions

1. Puree all the ingredients in a food processor until smooth.

2. Freeze the sorbet in 1 of 2 ways:

- Use an ice cream or sorbet maker and mix until the mixture thickens, around 25–30 minutes. Freeze until firm, around 2 hours.

- Pour the puree mixture into a shallow dish and put it in the freezer. Use a whisk to stir it every 15–20 minutes for about 2 hours so it won't freeze solid.

3. Serve the sorbet with a sprig of fresh mint.

Sail Away Tote

Finished Size: 13″ × 15½″

If you're like me, you can never have enough totes to tote things around in. This bag features two simple outer pockets inspired by the many sailboats out on the water this time of year.

Materials

Coordinating cotton fabrics:

Fabric 1 (main front and back panels): ½ yard

Fabric 2 (sail pocket 1 and straps): ⅝ yard

Fabric 3 (sail pocket 2 lining): ⅞ yard

Coordinating all-purpose sewing thread

Rotary cutter, ruler, and self-healing cutting mat

Sew-on hook-and-loop dots: 2 pairs

Fabric-marking pen (Always test on a scrap of fabric before using. I recommend FriXion pens.)

Shell buttons: 1 large (25mm) and 1 small (20mm)

Cutting

Fabric 1 (main front and back panels): Cut 2 rectangles 14″ × 17″.

Fabric 2 (sail pocket 1 and straps): Cut 1 rectangle 14″ × 17″ and 2 strips 2″ × 28″. (Feel free to cut the straps longer or shorter based on your preferences.)

Fabric 3 (sail pocket 2 lining): Cut 3 rectangles 14″ × 17″.

Shoe button
cut 2

Make It

Make the Main Tote Panels

Use a ½" seam allowance.

1. Position the sail pocket 1 fabric rectangle vertically on a cutting mat, right side up. Mark 7" up from the bottom left corner. Then mark 1" to the left of the top right corner. Place a straightedge so that it connects the 2 marks and then cut on the line with the rotary cutter.

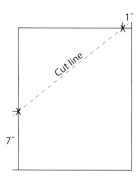

2. Position the sail pocket 2 fabric vertically on a cutting mat, right side up. Mark 3½" up from the bottom left corner. Next, mark ¾" to the left of the top right corner. Place a straightedge so that it connects the 2 marks and cut with the rotary cutter.

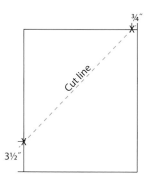

3. For both sail panels, fold back the raw edge of the diagonal line ¼" and press. Fold it back another ¼", press, and pin. Topstitch the top hem with a straight stitch.

4. For both sail panels, find the center point along each of the finished diagonal edges and mark it with a dot, just below the finished hem (on the wrong side of the fabric). Sew the fuzzy side of a hook-and-loop dot on the mark.

5. Following the illustration below, layer the front panel and both sail pockets, right sides up. Mark the fabric just below the fuzzy hook-and-loop dots. Sew the other halves of the hook-and-loop dots where you made the marks. One is sewn to the right side of the main panel, and the other dot is sewn to the right side of the sail 1 panel.

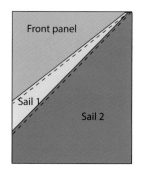

Dot on right side of front panel connects to dot on wrong side of sail 1.

Dot on right side of sail 1 connects to dot on wrong side of sail 2.

6. Layer the front panel and the sail pockets (all right sides up). Place the back panel right side down on top of the front sail layers. Carefully pin together.

7. Sew around the sides and bottom using a ½″ seam allowance. Trim the corners and any uneven edges to remove bulk; then turn the tote right side out. Press flat. Fold the top raw edge over 1″ toward the wrong side of the fabric and press.

Make the Lining

1. Place the lining panels right sides together and sew around the sides and bottom, using a ½″ seam allowance. Trim the corners and press flat. Fold the raw edges of the top over 1″ toward the wrong side of the lining fabric and press.

2. Slip the lining sack into the tote, wrong sides together, just like an envelope. Match up the folded tops of the outer tote and the lining. Press and pin in place.

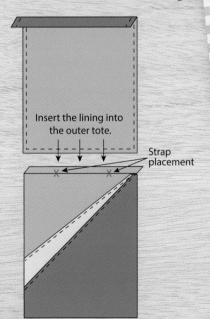

Insert the lining into the outer tote.

Strap placement

Add the Straps

1. Fold the straps in half lengthwise, wrong sides together, and press. Open the fold so that the fabric is wrong side up; then fold each raw edge in toward the center crease line. Press. Then fold in half again and press. Topstitch the entire length of both straps to finish them off. The straps now measure ½″ × 28″.

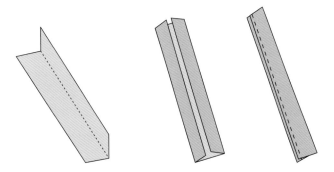

2. Place the tote on your work surface, front side facing up. Measure 3″ in from each side and make a mark. At the first mark, insert an inch of the end of a strap between the lining and exterior fabrics and pin in place. At the next mark, insert the other end of the strap in the same fashion and pin in place. Turn the tote over and repeat with the second strap on the other side. Sew around the top of the bag ½″ from the edge and again ¼″ from the top edge.

3. Finish your tote by hand sewing the buttons over the hook-and-loop dots for each of the sail pockets.

Voilà! You're ready to sail away!

Herbed New Potato Salad

Serves 4 • Preparation/cooking time: 20–30 minutes

There are two things that are *always* part of a Midsummer smorgasbord: strawberries and new potatoes. Eating some new potato salad on Midsummer is a tradition and celebrates the lovely new potatoes that are taking shape in the garden.

Ingredients

2 pounds new (baby) potatoes (or any variety available in your area)

2 tablespoons white wine vinegar

3 tablespoons extra virgin olive oil

3 spring onions, chopped

¼ cup flat-leafed parsley, chopped

Salt and pepper

Directions

1. Wash the potatoes and boil them in a large pot until they are tender but firm, approximately 15–20 minutes.

2. Drain the potatoes and let them cool in a large bowl. Gently toss the potatoes in the white wine vinegar, olive oil, onions, and parsley. Add salt and pepper to taste.

Seaside Picnic Quilt

Finished Size: 55½″ × 64½″

Contemplating laid-back summertime fun with friends at the beach makes for the perfect excuse to whip up a Seaside Picnic Quilt!

Materials

Fabric for quilt top: 2 yards quilting-weight cotton, light-weight upholstery fabric, or cotton bed linens (at least 60″ wide) with a large-scale print

Pocket fabric: 1¾ yards quilting-weight cotton

Backing fabric: 2 yards wide-width (60″) Gore-Tex (See Resources, page 110.)

Muslin, 90″ wide: 4 yards

Low-loft batting: 2 twin size (72″ × 90″)

Thread

Measuring tape and ruler

Fabric-marking pen (Always test on a scrap of fabric before using. I recommend FriXion pens.)

½″ bias tape (or other ribbon/strap material): 4¾ yards

Rotary cutter, clear Omnigrid ruler, and self-healing cutting mat

T square

A FEW NOTES ABOUT GORE-TEX

Using Gore-Tex was a bit of an experiment on my part, but I found it quite easy to work with.

- Gore-Tex *can* be machine washed on a warm permanent-press cycle (use light spinning and avoid wringing). Don't use fabric softeners, stain removers, or bleach, just a bit of gentle liquid detergent. No prewashing is needed.

- Line dry or tumble dry on warm/low temperature. If you've line dried it, you can reactivate the water repellency by drying it again on very low for 20 minutes.

- Iron on a warm setting with no steam. Place a pressing cloth between the Gore-Tex and the iron.

- Once you sew lots of tiny holes in it, it's probably more water resistant than water-proof. That being said, it's sure to stay dryer than 100% cotton.

Make It

Cutting

Wash, dry, and press the cotton fabric before you cut it. Trim off the selvages.

Quilt top: 58″ × 68″

Quilt top pocket: 58″ × 21″

Gore-Tex backing: 58″ × 68″

Batting: Cut 2 pieces 68″ × 78″ (Be sure to have enough to extend about 3″ beyond all sides of the quilt top and backing fabric.)

Muslin: Cut 2 pieces 68″ × 78″.

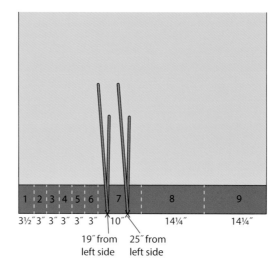

Make the Quilted Top and Back Panels

1. Using a fabric-marking pen and a ruler or T square, draw 1½″ (or any width you'd like) stripes across the width of the quilt top fabric.

2. Layer a 68″ × 78″ muslin piece, batting, and the fabric you chose for the quilt top, right side up. (The muslin and batting can be pressed if needed before layering and should extend beyond the top fabric several inches on all sides.) Pin the layers together carefully.

3. Sew over the lines you drew in Step 1 using a straight stitch.

4. Remove the fabric-marking pen marks according to the manufacturer's instructions. Trim off the excess batting and muslin. Square up the top so that it measures 58″ × 68″.

5. Repeat Steps 1–4 for the Gore-Tex backing.

Add the Pocket

1. Fold the pocket fabric in half lengthwise, wrong sides together, so that it measures 10½″ × 58″. Measure out the vertical stitch lines, which will create the pockets, with a ruler and fabric-marking pen. Line up the pocket fabric along the bottom of the quilt top (the raw edges of the pocket should line up with the raw edge of the quilt). Carefully pin the pocket in place.

2. Sew over the lines you drew to attach the pocket to the quilt top using a straight stitch.

Add the Straps

1. If you are using bias tape, stitch down the open side with a straight stitch close to the edge. Cut 2 pieces 72″ long.

2. Again, use a pen to mark the spots where you'll attach the straps. Measuring from left to right, make a mark at 19″ and another at 25″ (see illustration, page 70). One length of bias tape will be attached at each mark. Measure the bias tape 24″ from an end. Fold. The length on 1 side of the fold is 24″ and the length on the other side of the fold is 48″. Lay the strap on the quilt with the shorter length on top. The folds of the straps will be sewn into the seam at the bottom. Pin the folds of the straps to the marks you made at the bottom of the quilt top.

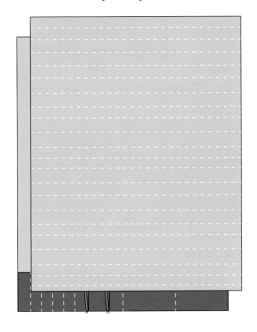

Finish It

1. Lay out the quilt front panel, right side up, with the straps pinned in place, and then lay the quilted back panel, right side down, on top of the quilt front. Line the sides up, making sure the straps are tucked in between the backing and the quilt top.

2. Pin the sides together securely; then stitch around the perimeter of the quilt with a ½″ seam allowance, leaving about 15″ open on a long side.

3. Trim the corners, being careful not to cut into the stitching. Turn the quilt inside out; then stitch the open area closed by folding in the seam allowance and stitching as close to the edge as you can (about ⅛″). Press flat.

4. Cut a 10″ piece of bias tape and overlap the ends by about 1½″; then stitch securely in place, making a handle "ring." Bring the 2 short straps through the ring you made and pull the ring close to the bottom seam of the quilt.

5. Slide some silverware wrapped in fabric napkins into the 3″ pockets and get ready to roll! Lay the quilt right side up. Spread the straps out so they extend away from the quilt. Fold both the right and left long sides in, with right sides together, so they meet at the center of the quilt. **FIGURE A**

Fold the side without straps over again, so it covers the section with the straps. The straps now extend from the bottom layer.
FIGURE B

6. From the end opposite the straps, begin rolling up the quilt. Bring the long strap around the bottom of the roll to meet up with the shorter strap. Make sure the loop is in place at the seam and then tie the long and short straps together with a tight bow. Cut the straps shorter if they are too long. Now head to the beach! **FIGURES C & D**

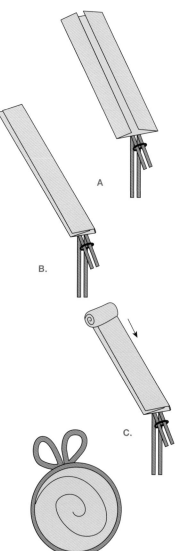

Beer-poached salmon is one of the easiest things in the world to make and is a classic Midsummer taste treat! Served up hot or cold with a cold brew, flat bread, fresh salad greens, and perhaps some new potato salad, too—you just can't go wrong.

Ingredients

2 pounds salmon fillets

1 microbrew or beer of your choice

Pinch salt

Pinch fresh cracked pepper

1 sprig fresh dill

1 lemon

Directions

ON THE CAMP STOVE (OR STOVE TOP)

1. Pour the beer into a deep skillet and bring to a simmer.

2. Add the salmon, making sure the beer nearly covers the fish.

3. Cover and simmer for 10–20 minutes, depending on how thick the fillets are—just enough so the fish is cooked through.

Dad's Beer-Poached Salmon

Serves 4 • Preparation/cooking time: ½ hour

IN THE OVEN

1. Preheat the oven to 425°.

2. Place the salmon in a deep baking dish; then pour enough beer over the fish to just barely cover it.

3. Cover the fish with foil and bake for 15–20 minutes (just enough so that the fish is cooked through).

Finishing

Garnish the fish with salt and fresh cracked pepper to taste, lemon wedges, and a sprig of fresh dill. Serve warm or cold with flat bread and lingonberry sauce (page 41).

Pocket Pals

Finished Size: Pocket: approximately 4″ × 4″; pals: 2″–3″ × 3″–3½″

Always have a friend in tow with a playful Pocket Pal. These pals travel well in their very own keepsake pocket. Take any simple outfit, attach a pocket with a pal inside, and away your little one goes!

Materials

Quilting-weight cotton: ⅛ yard, a fat eighth, or a fat quarter

Wool-blend felt: 1 sheet 12″ × 18″ each of a variety of colors for pals

Stuffing material: very small amount for each pal

All-purpose sewing thread in coordinating colors

8½″ × 11″ paper: 1 sheet for each template (pocket or pal)

Fabric-marking pen (Always test on a scrap of fabric before using. I recommend FriXion pens.)

Appliqué glue (I like Roxanne Glue-Baste-It.)

Hand-sewing and embroidery needles

Embroidery floss or crewel wool that coordinates with felt

Ribbon or rickrack, ¼″ or ½″ **wide:** 7″ for each pal

Sew-on hook-and-loop tape: ½″ × 2″ for each pal

Beads or buttons for embellishment (Caution: not for kids under 3 years)

Simple garment you want to put a pocket on

Make It

Make the Pocket

1. For the round pocket, trace the pattern (pullout page P1) onto a piece of paper and cut it out. With a fabric-marking pen, trace around the paper pattern on the fabric. Cut the fabric panel out. For the square pocket, cut a piece of fabric 4½″ × 8½″.

2. Sew the soft side of a hook-and-loop tape strip onto the front side of the pocket panel, as shown on the round pocket pattern (pullout page P1) or square pocket diagram (page 77).

3. Fold the pocket fabric in half, right sides together, and press lightly. Stitch around the perimeter of the pocket using a ¼″ seam allowance. Leave a 2″ section open on a side. For the round pocket, clip the curves, being careful not to cut into the stitching. For the square pocket, cut the corners, again being careful not to cut into the stitching. Turn the pocket right side out and press flat.

4. Place and pin the pocket on the garment where you'd like it to be (making sure the hook-and-loop tape is on the inside) and use a wide zigzag stitch around the sides and bottom of the pocket to attach it. The folded top is the pocket top.

Make the Pals

1. Trace the pattern pieces for 1 of the 7 pals (pages 79 and 80). Cut out the paper shapes and trace each shape onto the appropriate felt color. Cut 2 of each shape, making sure to note the numbers that go with each piece. Keep in mind when you make the back piece of each pal that the pattern needs to be flipped so it is the reverse of the front piece.

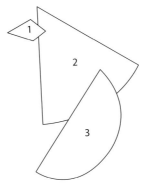

Cut second set of felt pieces on reverse.

2. Remove any marks from the fabric-marking pen according to the manufacturer's instructions. With a bit of appliqué glue, set each appliqué shape into position on the foundation layer. The appliqué shapes are numbered and glued down in numerical order.

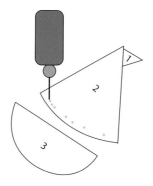

3. Hand stitch each appliqué piece in place with either embroidery floss or regular thread. Refer to the placement diagrams for decorative stitch locations and to Stitches (page 109) for how to do embroidery stitches. Add any beads or buttons if desired.

4. Carefully stitch or glue the ribbon or rickrack onto the back side of a pal panel. The ribbon or rickrack will end up being sandwiched between the 2 sides and inserted about 1″ inside.

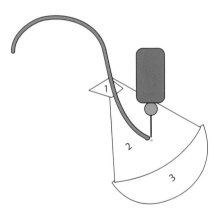

5. Once you've got the appliqué pieces and the ribbon securely in place, match up the front and back sides (right sides facing out) and stitch them together. Leave an opening for stuffing, add the stuffing, and then stitch the opening closed.

6. Sew the rough side of the hook-and-loop strip onto a 1½″ × 3″ piece of felt. Trim the felt, leaving ¼″ around the strip, making it 1″ × 2½″. Cut another piece of felt (without hook-and-loop tape) the same size (1″ × 2½″).

7. Sandwich the end of the ribbon or rickrack between the 2 rectangles of felt you just cut in Step 6. Make sure the rough hook-and-loop strip is facing out. Machine stitch around the felt, using a ¼″ seam allowance and securing the ribbon in the center of the felt. Trim the edges to about ⅛″ beyond the stitching line.

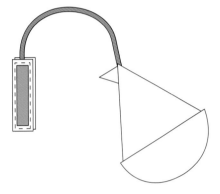

8. Attach the hook-and-loop strip of the ribbon to the hook-and-loop strip inside the pocket. Tuck the pal inside the pocket and have fun watching your little one show off his or her pal!

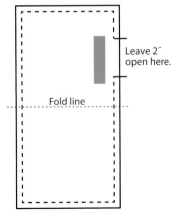

Leave 2″ open here.

Fold line

Square pocket

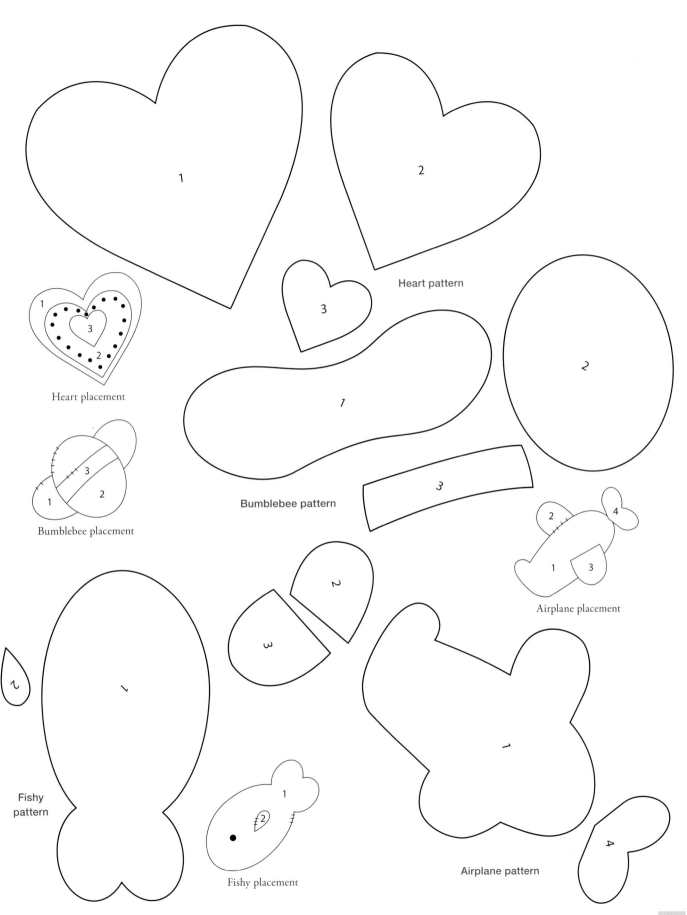

Heart pattern

Heart placement

Bumblebee pattern

Bumblebee placement

Airplane placement

Fishy pattern

Fishy placement

Airplane pattern

1

2V1

3V1

2V2

3V2

Flower pattern

2

1

3

Sailboat
pattern

1

Butterfly
pattern

1

2V1
3V1

1

2V2
3V2

Flower version 1
placement

Flower version 2
placement

2

3

4

5

1

2

3

5
4
4
5
3
1
4
2
4
5
3

Sailboat placement

Butterfly placement

Strawberries and Cream

Serves 4–6 • Preparation/cooking time: 15 minutes

Strawberries plus sweet cream. How simple is that? So simple we shun whipping cream from a can or plastic bucket!

Ingredients

Fresh strawberries—hulled, washed, and gently patted dry

---

1 cup heavy whipping cream—very cold

---

2 tablespoons powdered sugar (add to taste)

---

1 teaspoon vanilla extract

Directions

1. Pour the (cold) cream into a mixing bowl. Use a whisk (or hand mixer) and start adding the sugar and vanilla.

2. Continue to beat until firm, being careful not to overbeat.

Go Fish Mobile

Finished Size: Approximately 25″ × 28″

Watching fish swim is known to have a calming effect on a person's mood, so let's go fish! I list the lengths of the finished mobile strings just as a basic reference point. Don't worry about matching the exact measurements of the sample. There are no hard-and-fast rules here…just have fun with it!

Materials

Quilting cotton: 2 fat eighths in coordinating colors

fast2fuse HEAVY double-sided fusible interfacing: 1 sheet

Coordinating thread

8½″ × 11″ copier/printer paper: 1 sheet

Fabric-marking pen (Always test on a scrap of fabric before using. I recommend FriXion pens.)

¼″-diameter wooden dowel (4 lengths needed):

  A: 1 piece 13″

  B: 1 piece 9″

  C: 1 piece 6½″

  D: 1 piece 5″

Hand drill with ⁵⁄₆₄″ (0.078125″) drill bit

12-pound fishing line

Embroidery needle (with an eye big enough for the fishing line to go through)

Metal washers: various sizes (see Metal Washers, below)

CAUTION

This is a decorative mobile and is not meant to be used over a baby's crib or for small children younger than age 3.

METAL WASHERS

Find metal washers at your local hardware store. Washers come in a wide range of dimensions, and they also vary by the size of the center hole. Some are flat while others are beveled. I recommend picking up a few extras of each size, so you've got some flexibility in "weighting" each string. As a starting point, here's what I used. Most of the washers are beveled, and I measured across the outer circle.

1¾″—1 washer	⅞″—6 washers
1½″—1 washer	¾″—6 washers
1⅛″—7 washers	⅝″—8 washers

Make It

Make the Fabric Fish

1. Use the paper and a fabric-marking pen to trace the fish patterns (page 86) and then cut them out of the paper. Make 1 small fish template and 1 large fish template.

2. Lay a piece of fabric right side down on the ironing board; then place interfacing on top of it. Place the second piece of fabric right side up on top of the interfacing. Trim off excess fabric, but make sure the fabric pieces are ½″–1½″ bigger than the interfacing in the center. Follow the manufacturer's instructions to adhere the fabric to the interfacing.

3. Use the paper templates from Step 1 to trace 3 small fish and 2 large fish.

4. Have some fun quilting the fish by sewing waves of stitches. Just move the fish sandwich panel in a wavy motion as you run it through the machine. Keep going until you have quilted the entire surface.

5. Cut out the quilted fish shapes. Zigzag stitch around the perimeter of each fish to finish the raw edges and tie off the threads with a simple knot. Thread the loose thread ends onto a hand-sewing needle and pull them through the body of the fish. Remove any leftover pen marks according to the manufacturer's instructions. Your fish are ready to swim—or fly!

Prep the Wood Dowels

Take out the wooden dowels and the power drill. If you've never used a drill before, get some expert assistance—it's not difficult, but any power tool can be dangerous if you don't know how to use it carefully. Don't forget your safety glasses! You will be drilling 3 holes into each dowel: 2 that are ¼″ away from each cut end and a third exactly in the center. Make a dot with a pen where you'll drill; then drill the holes.

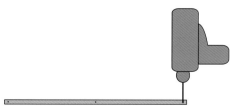

Connect the Pieces

1. You'll need to have a large flat surface to work on (a dining room table usually does the trick). Follow the mobile map (page 85) to plan out where to put the washers, fish, and dowels in relationship to each other.

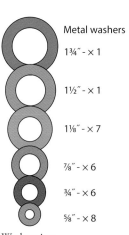

Metal washers

1¾″ - × 1

1½″ - × 1

1⅛″ - × 7

⅞″ - × 6

¾″ - × 6

⅝″ - × 8

Washer sizes

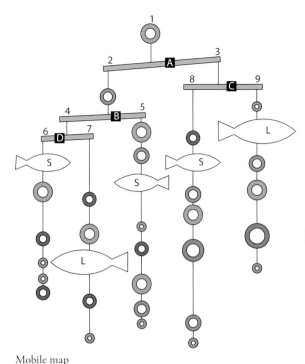

Mobile map

2. Start from the bottom up. Begin by connecting the washers and fish with fishing line. Use a double half hitch knot (page 86) to connect each piece. Make all 5 washer and fish strings.

Approximate finished lengths on the mobile map are:

Line 1: 3″

Line 2: 4½″

Line 3: 3″

Line 4: 1¾″

Line 5: 19″

Line 6: 14″

Line 7: 18″

Line 8: 22″

Line 9: 15″

3. Start connecting the wooden dowels to the strings you've strung. Be mindful of the distances between the dowels and the other elements. You want just enough room so

that all the pieces can float freely without bumping into each other. Thread the fishing line through the hole several times. You can come up over both sides of the dowel to wrap it with the fishing line.

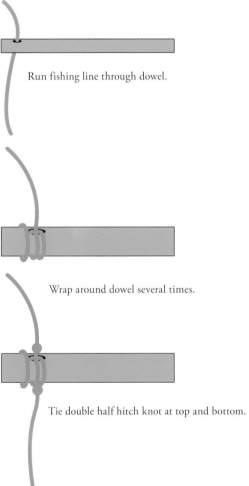

Run fishing line through dowel.

Wrap around dowel several times.

Tie double half hitch knot at top and bottom.

4. Tie the fishing line off with a double half hitch knot and another regular knot for good measure. Trim off the extra fishing line at the knot without cutting too close to the actual knot (leave about ¼″). Keep going until all the elements are attached.

How to Tie a Double Half Hitch Knot

A double half hitch knot is what we'll use to secure each length of fishing line to the metal washers, quilted fish, and wooden dowels.

1. Bring the fishing line through the washer, fish, or dowel. Pass the end you just brought through the washer over the remaining end (or the standing end) of the fishing line. Bring the loose end back up and through the loop you just made; then pull it tight to complete the first half hitch.

2. Pass the end over the standing part of the fishing line again. Bring the end back up and through the second loop you just formed, making the second half hitch; then tighten it up.

That's it! You've just made a double half hitch knot. Way to go, sailor!

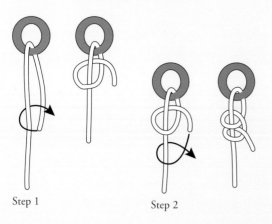

Step 1   Step 2

5. Now the moment of truth. … Carefully lift up the mobile from the top washer. If there are any unbalanced parts, you can add washers here and there until it's balanced out. Find a sunny spot to hang it and enjoy watching your happy fish swim in the air. Remember, it's good for you!

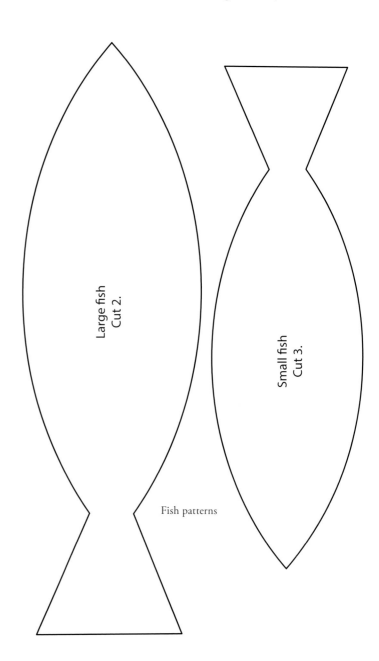

Large fish
Cut 2.

Small fish
Cut 3.

Fish patterns

Fabric Flower Swag

Finished Size: 3″ × 52½″ (with 4″ metal rings)

Nothing says summer more than fresh-picked (or, in our case, fabric) flowers. Flowers are a welcome sign that the warm weather celebrations are here! On Midsummer's Eve, it's a tradition to start the day by picking as many fresh flowers as you can carry to decorate wreaths, a maypole, and the house. This floral swag is a great way to bring friends and family together to celebrate the season—it becomes a real flower factory when there's more than one of you making these! Your fabric flower swag can be hung on an entry door or a wall or used as a table runner—indoors or out.

Materials

Medium-weight white linen or linen-blend fabric: ¼ yard of 55″- to 60″-wide fabric OR 1¾ yard of 42″- to 45″-wide fabric

Quilting-weight cotton: ¼ yard or 1 fat quarter each of 7 colors: bright green, dark green, yellow, yellow-orange, orange, dark orange, blue

White quilting-weight cotton: ½ yard

Iron-on adhesive: 2 yards (I used HeatnBond Feather Lite.)

All-purpose sewing thread in coordinating colors

Measuring tape and ruler

Fabric-marking pen (Always test on a scrap of fabric before using. I recommend FriXion pens.)

8½″ × 11″ printer/copier paper: 2 sheets

Rotary cutter and self-healing cutting mat

T square

Hand-sewing needle

Beads, buttons, or other embellishments for flower centers (I used white glass and wood beads, along with some small wood buttons.)

Sink strainer locknuts, 4″: 2 (Feel free to use any kind of "ring" about 4″ in diameter that you think will work. Explore your local hardware store—you might be surprised what you can use!)

DANCING AROUND THE MAYPOLE

The Midsummer pole is a symbol of abundance and fertility and is the first thing to be decorated on (or just prior to) Midsummer's Eve. Then it is paraded around before being set up on the green (whether it be a public park or a backyard) for the night's festivities. It's pretty typical to see people wearing traditional costumes and dancing their way around a Midsummer pole! If you catch anyone dancing around a maypole in the buff … chances are good they are having a great time—and maybe have said "*Skol!*" ("More schnapps!") one too many times.

Make It

Cutting

Press the cotton fabric before you cut it. Trim off the selvages. There's no need to prewash your fabric for this project.

Linen: 4½″ × 54½″

Quilting-weight cotton fabric: Cut each piece in half width-wise and separate into 2 stacks.

FLOWER POWER

Flowers and herbs collected this time of year are said to bring prosperity and good health, so decorating your home (or your hair) with flowers and greenery is a must. Flower swags not only decorate doors and tables, but also decorate "Midsummer poles" (or maypoles).

The flower structure starts by using iron-on adhesive to join two pieces of fabric. I've found this gives the flowers form without making them too stiff. Additionally, you can combine two different colors of fabric, which allows you to make two-tone flowers.

Here's a basic list of how many flowers to make. Feel free to use whichever flowers and sizes you want from the four flower types in the patterns (pages 92 and 93). You may end up having a few left over or decide you want to add more in.

- 8 large white daisies
- 12 large poppies (in a variety of yellow/orange colors)
- 12 small poppies (in 2 different yellow/orange colorways)
- 12 large zinnias (in a variety of yellow/orange colors)
- 12 small zinnias (in a variety of yellow/orange colors)
- 6 tiny white zinnias
- 12 blue starflowers

1. Apply iron-on adhesive to the back side of each fabric piece from 1 stack. First, place the appliqué fabric right side down on the ironing board. Place the iron-on adhesive on top, paper side up. Make sure your fabric is slightly larger than the paper template. Use a pressing cloth to avoid getting adhesive and ink on your iron.

2. Place adhesive-backed fabric on the ironing board, adhesive side up. From the second stack, place a fabric piece on top, right side up. Press to adhere. I put white on white, blue on white, bright green on dark green (for the leaves), yellow on yellow-orange, and orange on dark orange. Feel free to mix up your flower petal fabric any way you choose.

3. Trace only the solid lines of the flower patterns (pages 92 and 93) onto a sheet of paper; then cut out the basic shapes.

4. Trace the flower patterns onto the prepared fabric with a fabric-marking pen and cut them out. Remove any fabric pen marks from the basic shapes you cut out. Refer to the illustrated pattern again to finish cutting the flower petals. You will also see how to combine the shapes for each flower and where to "pinch" the petals and leaves to give them form.

5. After you have all the flower parts cut and paired up, layer the appropriate flower parts together (with a leaf or 2) and bring your threaded needle up (from the back)

through the center of the layers. Thread a bead or button at the top. Pull the needle back through all the layers and the bead or button a few times; then tie the thread off with a knot on the back. Continue to assemble all of the flowers.

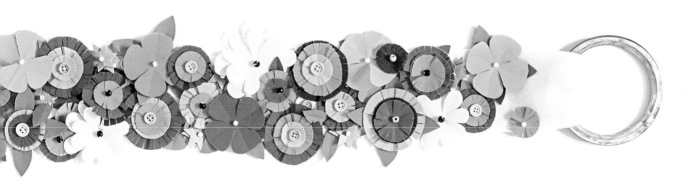

Finish It

1. Finish the sides of the linen panel you cut. Fold over each long side ¼″ and press. Fold over each long side again ½″ and press. Topstitch with a straight stitch to secure the finished sides.

2. Fold back each of the short ends ¼″ and press. Then pull each short end through a metal ring (1 on each end). Fold the fabric 4″ over to the back and sew with a straight stitch to secure it.

3. Hand stitch the flowers in place onto the swag. The simplest way to do this is to start with the biggest flowers, spacing them out down the swag, and then fill in the spaces as you go. When you're happy with the flower placement, you're done! Simple as that!

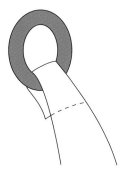

Daisy patterns. Cut on dashed lines.

Zinnia patterns. Cut on dashed lines.

Starflower patterns. Cut on dashed lines.

Poppy patterns. Cut on dashed lines.
Crease on solid gray lines.

Leaf patterns. Crease on solid gray lines.

Fabric Flower Swag

Sheer Pillow Wraps

Finished Size: For 20″ × 20″ pillow: 9″ × 36″ or 12″ × 36″; for 18″ × 18″ pillow: 9″ × 34″

Wrap a fresh summer look over pillows you already have with these sheer appliquéd pillow wraps!

Materials

Cotton voile fabric: 1 yard

Coordinating ¼″ or ½″ ribbon: 2¼″ yards

White all-purpose sewing thread

White gift-wrapping tissue paper

Iron-on adhesive (lite): 1 yard

Fabric-marking pen (Always test on a scrap of fabric before using. I recommend FriXion pens.)

Felt-tipped permanent marker

8½″ × 11″ printer/copier paper

Rotary cutter and self-healing cutting mat

Hand-sewing needle

Beads or buttons for embellishing

Optional but Helpful

⅛″ graph paper (This paper helps you place the appliqués for the stripe and square grid designs. You can find a graph paper pattern online and print it (see Resources, page 110). Make sure you find paper that is eight lines per inch.

Note: Before cutting the appliqué fabric, apply iron-on adhesive to the back of each appliqué piece that's at least 11″ × 11″. Remove the paper from the iron-on adhesive; then follow the cutting directions (page 96).

Make It

Cutting

18″ × 18″ pillow (stripe design):

Wrap: Cut 1 piece 10″ × 35″.

Appliqués: Cut 3 rectangles 2″ × 10″ and 2 rectangles 1″ × 10″.

20″ × 20″ pillow (oval design):

Wrap: Cut 1 piece 13″ × 37″.

Appliqués: Use the pattern (page 98) to trace the oval onto a piece of paper. Cut out the paper template and, using a fabric-marking pen, trace 3 ovals onto the appliqué fabric. Cut out the fabric appliqués.

20″ × 20″ pillow (5 × 5 square grid design):

Wrap: Cut 1 piece 13″ × 37″.

Appliqués: Cut 25 squares 1¾″ × 1¾″.

20″ × 20″ pillow (4 × 3 square grid design):

Wrap: Cut 1 piece 10″ × 37″.

Appliqués: Cut 12 squares 1¾″ × 1¾″.

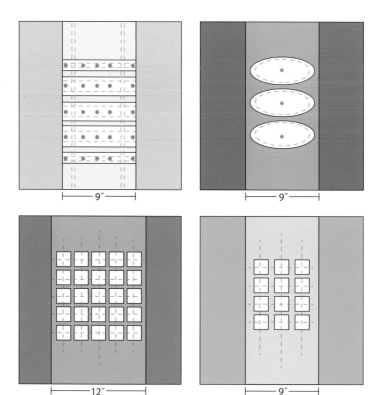

Make the Grid Map

If you are using graph paper, use a permanent marker to draw dark lines on the graph paper, mapping out either the square grid design or the stripes as follows:

SQUARE GRID

25 squares 1¾″ × 1¾″ (5 rows of 5 across), evenly spaced, ⅜″ apart from each other

SQUARE GRID

12 squares 1¾″ × 1¾″ (4 rows of 3 across), evenly spaced, ¾″ apart

STRIPES

A 1″-wide stripe is followed by 3 stripes 2″ wide and then 1 more stripe 1″ wide at the bottom. There are ½″ spaces between the stripes.

Iron the Appliqué Shapes

FOR THE SQUARE OR STRIPE DESIGNS:

1. Find the center point of the pillow wrap foundation fabric (the area that will be visible on the pillow top).

2. Put the graph paper you just drew under the fabric, which should be right side up.

3. Remove the paper backing from the appliqués. Place the appliqué pieces (right side up, adhesive side down) on top of the wrap panel, following the placement of the graph paper. Iron the appliqué shapes in place.

FOR THE OVAL DESIGN:

1. Find the center point of the pillow wrap foundation fabric (the area that will be visible on the pillow top).

2. Remove the paper backing from the appliqués. Place the appliqué pieces (right side up, adhesive side down) on top of the wrap panel. Center an oval and place the other 2 on either side (as shown in the Stitch It, Step 2 illustration, below) and then iron them in place.

Stitch It

1. Finish the raw edges by folding each of the long sides of the wrap over ¼″ toward the back and press. Fold over ¼″ again and press. Pin to keep the sides folded over and then topstitch the fold, just under ¼″ from the edge.

2. Lay out a smoothed-flat piece of tissue paper under the wrap panel. (Note: The tissue paper can be pressed flat with the steam setting off, if necessary.) Make sure the tissue covers the entire appliqué area. Securely pin the fabric to the tissue paper with the appliqués as flat as possible.

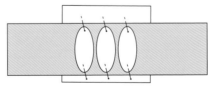

TIP

The tissue paper acts as a nonslippery base under the very lightweight sheer fabric, making sewing easier. It helps keep the fabric flat and prevents puckering.

3. Sew down the appliqué pieces using a straight stitch. Carefully remove the tissue from the stitching on the back side.

Finish It

1. Add ribbon ties to the short ends of the pillow wrap. Cut ribbon into 6 pieces 12″ long for each pillow wrap. Fold the short ends of the wrap over ¼″ and press. Insert a ribbon on each corner and another in the center. Fold the ribbon and the short side of the fabric over again and pin it to secure the folds and the ribbon placement. Topstitch over the fold and the ribbon.

2. Embellish with beads, buttons, or something totally unique. Give the wrap a bit of steam pressing, wrap it around your pillow and tie it on the back, and you're done!

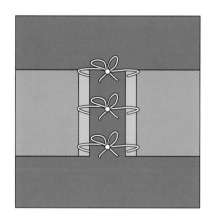

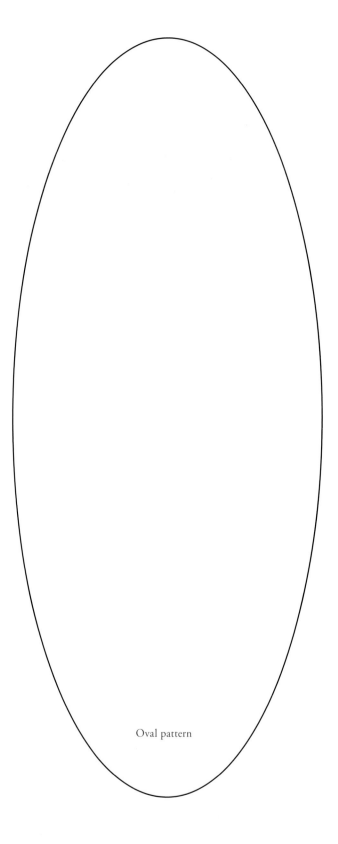

Oval pattern

Quilted Bed Scarf

Finished Size: 13″ × 80″

Lighten up in the summer by taking off the extra-warm bedding of winter and replacing it with a quilted scarf instead. Simple to make; simple to use.

Materials

Linen or linen/cotton-blend fabric: 1¼ yards (54″ wide) for top (I used a natural oat color.)

Linen or linen/cotton-blend fabric: 2½ yards for backing and appliqué (I used white.)

Muslin: 2¾ yards

Low-loft batting: Twin size

Iron-on adhesive: 1 yard (I used Heat*n*Bond Feather Lite.)

All-purpose sewing thread in coordinating colors

Measuring tape and ruler

Fabric-marking pen (Always test on a scrap of fabric before using. I recommend FriXion pens.)

Rotary cutter and self-healing cutting mat

T square

Embroidery needle

Large buttons: 3 (I used dark-stained wood buttons.)

Embroidery floss: 1 skein (I used dark brown crewel wool.)

Cutting

Wash, dry, and press the fabric before you cut it.
Trim off the selvages.

Panel A

Top fabric: 18″ × 45″

Batting: 22″ × 49″

Muslin: 22″ × 49″

Panel B

Top fabric: 18″ × 25″

Batting: 22″ × 29″

Muslin: 22″ × 29″

Appliqué fabric: 9″ × 21″

Panel C

Top fabric: 18″ × 25″

Batting: 22″ × 29″

Muslin: 22″ × 29″

Backing

Backing fabric: 14″ × 81″

Make It

Make Appliqué Panel B

1. Press iron-on adhesive to the back of the fabric you intend to use for the appliqué that will be adhered to panel B. Place the appliqué fabric right side down on the ironing board. Place the iron-on adhesive on top, paper side up. Make sure your fabric is slightly larger than the pattern will be. Use a pressing cloth to avoid getting adhesive and ink on your iron. Remove the paper backing from the adhesive after the fabric has cooled.

2. Trace the oval pattern (page 98) onto paper; then cut out the template. With a fabric-marking pen, trace 3 centered and evenly spaced ovals on the right side of the appliqué fabric panel. Cut out the center of the ovals from the appliqué.

3. Center the appliqué (right side up, adhesive side down) on panel B (also right side up). Iron the appliqué to panel B. Use a pressing cloth.

4. Sew a zigzag stitch around any raw edges of the appliqué (except the sides that will be sewn into the seam allowance). With an embroidery needle, thread the loose ends of the zigzag stitches and bring them to the back of the panel. Tie them off with a knot.

5. Use a fabric-marking pen to draw horizontal quilting lines across the panel top. See the quilting diagram for stitching.

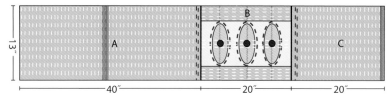

Quilting

6. Layer the muslin, batting, and panel B top in that order, on top of each other. The muslin and batting should extend about 2″ beyond the top panel. Pin the layers together and then use a straight stitch to sew over the lines you drew. Cut off excess batting and muslin and square up the panel to measure 14″ × 21″. Remove any remaining pen marks according to the manufacturer's instructions.

Make Panels A and C

1. With a fabric-marking pen and T square, draw vertical lines spaced ½″ apart from short side to short side, along the entire length of both panels A and C.

2. Layer the muslin, batting, and panel A, and a second set for panel C, in that order, on top of each other. The muslin and batting should extend about 2″ beyond each panel. Pin together and quilt on the drawn lines. Cut off the excess batting and muslin and square up the panels so that panel A measures 14″ × 41″ and panel C measures 14″ × 21″.

3. Following the manufacturer's instructions, remove any remaining pen marks. Add a few lines of embroidery (see the quilting diagram, page 102, for placement). I backstitched (see Stitches, page 109) with a double strand of crewel wool.

Piece the Top Panels

Use a ½″ seam allowance unless otherwise noted.

1. Place panels A and B right sides together, matching up a short 14″ side. Sew together.

2. Match up the raw 14″ side of panel B with a 14″ side of panel C, with right sides together. Sew together.

3. Press the back seams open; then flip the piece over so it's right side up again. Topstitch ¼″ along each side of the seams. This gives it a nice finished look and ensures that the opened seam will stay in place during finishing.

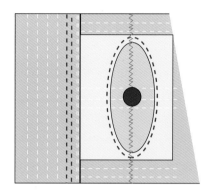

Finish It

1. Lay out the backing fabric and place the finished quilt top on top, right sides together. Smooth everything out, square it up once again, and carefully pin it all the way around.

2. Stitch around all 4 sides, but leave open a 8″–10″ gap along a long side.

3. Trim off the corners, being careful not to cut into the stitching, and turn the quilt right side out. Fold the open seam allowance to the inside and stitch it closed as close to the seam's edge as possible. Press flat.

4. Stitch the buttons onto the center points of the ovals, and there you have it!

Breezy Appliquéd Curtains

Finished Size: Varies (size will be determined by your window measurements)

Let the summer breeze softly drift in with these sheer curtains. Appliquéd using soft, semisheer batiste in the colors of well-worn sea glass, they will make your room feel like a summer beach house.

NOTE

The materials listed are based on the curtain I made—so just be aware that the measurements and materials will be different based on your window measurements and the width of the fabric.

Materials

To make a single panel:

100% cotton voile, 54″–56″ wide: 2½ yards

Batiste: ¼ yard or 1 fat quarter each of 4 soft colors

All-purpose sewing thread in coordinating colors

White gift-wrapping tissue paper

Fabric-marking pen (Always test on a scrap of fabric before using. I recommend FriXion pens.)

T square (or other straight-edge ruler)

Right-angle ruler

Rotary cutter and self-healing cutting mat

Embroidery floss that coordinates with appliqué fabrics (I used 4 colors.)

Embroidery needle and threader

Shell or wood buttons

Cutting

Wash, dry, and press the fabric before you cut it to preshrink it.

1. Cut the main curtain panel using the measurements you determine in Measure the Window (page 106).

2. Cut a strip 1″ × the width of the fabric panel.

Measure the Window

Measure the size of the window you want to cover:

- Your window width measurement is equal to the width of your window plus the amount needed to cover the window casings. If you already have a rod in place, your window width is equal to the length of the rod.

- Your window width + 5″ = cut width

- Your window height measurement equals the number of inches from the curtain rod to the floor.

- Your window height + 6½″ = cut length

Make It

Make the Curtain Panel

1. Finish the sides of the curtain panel by folding back each length's raw edge ½″ and pressing. Fold each side over again 1″, press, and pin in place. Topstitch each of the sides with a straight stitch.

2. Finish the top by folding back the raw edge ½″ and pressing. Fold it over again 2″, press, and pin in place. Stitch along the inner fold to create a pocket for the curtain rod. You can also use curtain rings with clips if you prefer.

3. Time to check the length and measure where you want the appliqués to go. Hang up the curtain by inserting the curtain rod through the top pocket (or by clipping the curtain to the curtain rings if you're using that method). Measure the distance from the top of the curtain to the windowsill. Make a note of this measurement and mark it with your fabric-marking pen. Next, fold up the bottom hem so it's just above the floor. Make a note of how many inches the hem needs to be; then put a pin at the point of the fold to mark it.

4. Take down the curtain from the rod and fold over the raw edge of the bottom hem ½″ and press. Fold it over again at the point you folded it up to in Step 3, press it flat, and stitch the hem in place.

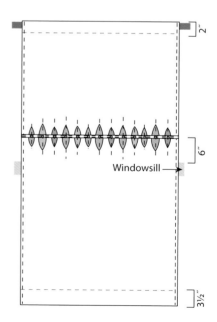

Appliqué

1. With a fabric-marking pen, make a horizontal line across the entire width of the curtain panel, 6″ above the windowsill measurement mark made in Make the Curtain Panel, Step 3 (page 106).

2. Trace the appliqué pattern (pullout page P2) onto the paper. Lay a piece of appliqué fabric over the tracing and use a fabric-marking pen to trace all the shapes onto the appropriate colors of appliqué fabric. I ended up using 19 appliqués across our curtain panel. Cut out all the fabric appliqué shapes.

3. Place the appliqué shapes vertically along the horizontal line you drew in Step 1. As you place the appliqués, mix up the colors and the sizes of the shapes, spacing them out evenly (about 1″ apart). Use a right-angle ruler to ensure that they are vertical and pin them onto the curtain panel.

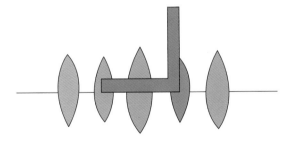

4. Lay out a smoothed-flat piece of tissue paper under the appliquéd area of the curtain panel. (Note: The tissue paper can be pressed flat with the steam setting off, if necessary.) Pin the paper, fabric panel, and appliqués together; then sew a straight stitch around each of the appliqués, ¼″ from the raw edge. Carefully remove the tissue paper from the back of the curtain panel.

5. Place the 1″ strip across the center horizontal line and center it across all the appliqués. Fold the ends over at each of the finished sides of the curtain panel. Add tissue to the back side of the appliquéd area of the curtain panel again (you can add sections of tissue about 4″ wide across the entire width of the fabric for this step). Topstitch the strip in place twice (¼″ from each of the raw edges).

Embroider

1. Lay out the curtain panel right side up. Use a fabric-marking pen and right-angle ruler to draw vertical lines through the top and bottom points of each appliqué. Draw a variety of lengths for these lines.

2. Embroider along each of the vertical lines you drew over the appliqués with a running stitch and add a French knot at the top and bottom of the stitching. (See Stitches, page 109.)

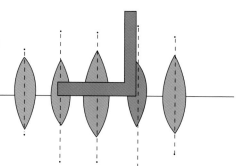

3. Add a shell or wooden button to the center of each appliqué.

4. Remove any remaining pen marks according to the manufacturer's instructions and finish pressing the curtain panel. Make a second panel, if desired. Hang up your new curtains and let the summer breezes flow!

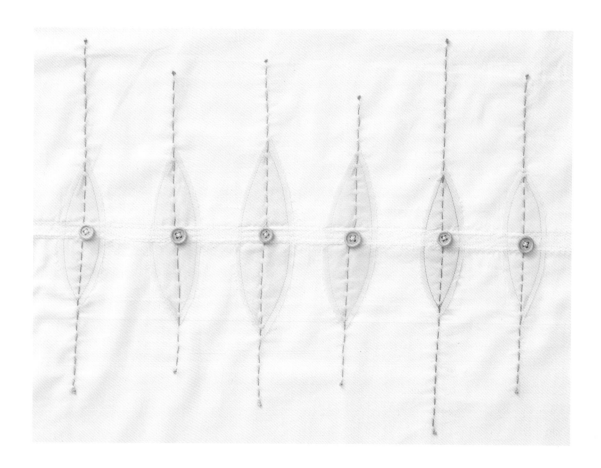

Stitches

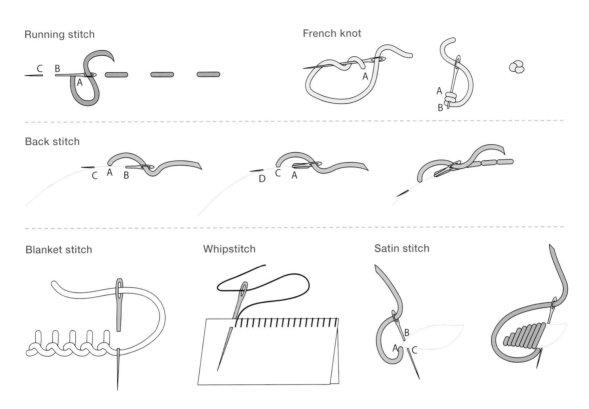

Running stitch

French knot

Back stitch

Blanket stitch

Whipstitch

Satin stitch

About the Author

Photo by Wes Cogan

In first grade, Kirstyn got on a bus she didn't normally get on—on purpose, just to see where it would go. Having survived that ordeal (and her parents' reaction), she has carried that same sense of adventure into her creative path, not always knowing where "that bus" would lead, but staying the creative course anyway. It was her time spent as a staff artist in the garment industry and a push from her dear friend Jane to go to Quilt Market that led her to begin designing appliqué, embroidery, and simple sewing projects.

Kirstyn's love of Scandinavian design stems from the midcentury Danish furniture and other miscellaneous Scandinavian artifacts her folks collected along life's way, as well as her visits to Sweden and Finland (and her own Scandinavian roots). Her work has appeared on greeting cards and stationery, picture frames and photo albums, quilting fabric and clothing for companies large and small. Her studio is now in Seattle, where she lives with her rockin' keyboard-playing husband, Wes. Contact Kirstyn at kirstyncogan.com.

Resources

FAVORITE TOOLS

Here's a list of tools I *love* and use in my studio *all* the time. They were used extensively in making the projects featured in this book.

FRIXION PENS

I can't live without FriXion pens—best thing since sliced bread.

pilotpen.us > Brands > FriXion > FriXion Ball Clicker

OLISO PRO IRON

I'll say it again … I love this iron.

www.oliso.com/quickshop > Oliso Pro Smart Iron with iTouch Technology TG1600

METAL T SQUARE AND RIGHT-ANGLE RULER

These can be found at art supply and office supply stores. A T square and a right-angle ruler just make squaring up projects that much easier.

CRYSTAL GLASS-HEAD PINS

You will never go back to using plastic-head pins after you start using these. Not only are the points of the pins sharper, but you can iron over them and they won't melt!

FABRICS

The fabrics used in the quilts and projects in this book were produced by the following manufacturers:

IKEA
ikea.com

MICHAEL MILLER FABRICS
michaelmillerfabrics.com

MODA   unitednotions.com

P&B TEXTILES   pbtex.com

ROBERT KAUFMAN
robertkaufman.com

WESTMINSTER FABRICS
westminsterfabrics.com

WINDHAM FABRICS
windhamfabrics.com

GORE-TEX

Check some of your local shops for Gore-Tex by the yard. Here are some online sources:

ROCKYWOODS FABRICS   rockywoods.com
OUTDOOR WILDERNESS FABRICS   owfinc.com/fabrics
SPECIALTY OUTDOORS   specialtyoutdoors.com

FELT AND WOOL

WEEKS DYE WORKS
weeksdyeworks.com
NATIONAL NONWOVENS
nationalnonwovens.com
PRAIRIE WOOLENS
prairiewoolens.com
AMERICAN FELT AND CRAFT
feltandcraft.com

COTTON VOILE AND BATISTE
fabric.com

MORE SCANDINAVIAN FABRIC
MARIMEKKO   us.marimekko.com
THE SWEDISH FABRIC COMPANY
(UK based)
theswedishfabriccompany.com

OTHER SUPPLIES

DILL BUTTONS (The buttons in this book were provided by Dill.)
us.dill-buttons.com

FAST2FUSE HEAVY (double-sided fusible interfacing)
ctpub.com > Tools & Notions > Interfacing > fast2fuse

QUILTERS DREAM BATTING   quiltersdreambatting.com

FAIRFIELD (American Spirit Classic Cotton Batting)
fairfieldworld.com > Our Products > Quilt Batting

HEATNBOND FEATHER LITE (iron-on adhesive)   thermowebonline.com >
Sewing & Quilt > Iron-On Fabric Adhesives > Sewable - Feather Lite

ROXANNE GLUE-BASTE-IT   colonialneedle.com

FISKARS SCISSORS, ROTARY CUTTERS, AND CUTTING MAT
fiskars.com

OMNIGRID RULERS (also cutting tools and mats)
prym-consumer-usa.com

PRINTABLE GRAPH PAPER   printablepaper.net > Graph Paper

SCANDINAVIAN COOKING AND INSPIRATION

INGEBRETSEN'S   ingebretsens.com

This is the Scandinavian specialty store my grandmother would take me to when I was a kid. It's still there, better than ever.

NORTHWEST WILDFOODS   nwwildfoods.com > Wild Berries

SCANDINAVIAN SPECIALTIES   scanspecialties.com

NORSLAND LEFSE   norslandlefse.com

SCANDINAVIAN FOOD STORE   scandinavianfoodstore.com

IKEA   ikea.com/us/en > Food

AMERICAN-SCANDINAVIAN FOUNDATION   amscan.org

NORDIC HERITAGE MUSEUM   nordicmuseum.org

SCANDINAVIAN HERITAGE ASSOCIATION   scandinavianheritage.org

stashBOOKS®

fabric arts for a handmade lifestyle

If you're craving beautiful authenticity in a time of mass-production...Stash Books is for you. Stash Books is a line of how-to books celebrating fabric arts for a handmade lifestyle. Backed by C&T Publishing's solid reputation for quality, Stash Books will inspire you with contemporary designs, clear and simple instructions, and engaging photography.

ctpub.com